the Art of DEATH MIDWIFERY

An Introduction and Beginner's Guide

JOELLYN ST. PIERRE, D. DIV.

ISBN: 1-4392-2906-6
ISBN-13: 9781439229064

Visit www.booksurge.com to order additional copies.

*For **John** – Sounds like a dare to me.*

*For **Maggie** – My first teacher.*

*And for my husband **Richard** – You are my rock.*

TABLE OF CONTENTS

ACKNOWLEDGEMENTS

No work is a solitary effort, and this one is no exception. None of what I do is without the aid and guidance of "the team," and to them I am eternally grateful. It is their inspiration that informs this book and this art.

I stand upon the shoulders of those who came before me, those whose work inspired me to walk this path. My deepest gratitude goes to Elizabeth Kubler-Ross and Anya Foos-Graber, two women who stood on the other side of the abyss, calling out gently in the dark, and midwifed me into this new life.

To Jae Malone; your skill and dedication as editor are greatly appreciated.

To my husband, Richard, who has lifted me up throughout the entire birthing of, not only this book, but of all the work of this path, I love you and thank you. You are a willing partner in this adventure; and I knew when we met that you were a vital piece, which up to that point had been missing. Thank you, as well, for taking the photos and creating the diagrams for this book.

To my spiritual mentor, Joseph Lee: I give great thanks for all of your inspiration, wise counsel and for the use of your poem for this book. Without your push, none of this may have come to fruition. Thanks, Joseph, for "pouring alcohol on the fire."

Thanks also go to my soul family, the members of the Mystery School, for all the support and insights you've so graciously given.

To all the students in our workshops, thank you, as well. A teacher learns as much from her students as she, hopefully, gives. I continue to learn from you all.

To all the people who have allowed me to commune with them in that most transformational process we call death, I thank you. It is an honor to be in your presence.

To my mother, father, friends, and all of the people I worked with in my years as a professional singer/dancer/actress in theatre and lost: Know that your deaths brought me to the place where I am today. Each of your transitions shaped and molded me into a death midwife.

To Maggie Mae, my beloved dog and first teacher: I hope all the work that's flowed from your passing makes up for my complete inexperience at the time.

And, finally, to John Lee Williams: You were the consummate pianist and artist. Your death was my initiation onto this path of service. It is in your name that I dedicate not only this book, but also whatever good may come from the art of death midwifery. With your death came the end of the art we created together…in that form. Now it is reborn in this new form…and once more it is a duet. Play on, John. Play on!

Note to Our Dear Readers

The art of death midwifery can be learned and practiced by both women and men. Not being a subscriber to "political correctness," and to honor the role performed exclusively by women in ancient cultures, I choose to keep the term in its feminine. Also, in order to become a spiritual death midwife, one must access and work with sensitivities and sensibilities, such as intuition and empathy, considered "feminine" in most spiritual traditions. Throughout the book, you will notice that I alternate references to the death midwife as he or she, to stress the point that this path of service is not gender exclusive.

In making references to God, you will notice many different terms being used. The art of death midwifery honors all spiritual traditions and philosophies and, therefore, seeks to be inclusive in terminology. Please substitute whatever name for the Higher Power of your understanding that feels most potent to you.

There are many levels to this practice. Although this book is focused on those who wish to go more deeply into this path of service, it is our hope that everyone can find something useful in these pages.

Many names have been changed to protect confidentiality. John and Michael are the only people whose names haven't been changed. I know that John doesn't mind. Michael's death was widely reported in newspapers throughout the U.S. so I do not feel mentioning him by first name violates his family's privacy.

This book is the collaborative effort between my "team" and me, so the use of the pronouns "I" or "we" are interchanged throughout. Hopefully that will not cause confusion.

INTRODUCTION

This book is the result of more than 18 years of service to the dying. It is based on my own personal work, research, and experimentation. There are many ways to serve the dying, and respect should be paid to all. In my many years of hospice work, however, I yearned to create a deeper and more profound way to assist and commune with the dying. After exhausting all my external resources, I turned inward. Through deep inner work, piece by piece, The Art of Death Midwifery began to surface.

Although there are many worthy schools that teach various forms of energy work and healing, the art I offer to you in this book comes from my inner teachers. They are my inspiration.

There are many techniques for invoking divine light. Though I do not claim to be an expert in them all, I have noticed the techniques tend to fall into two categories: those that draw from both personal and divine source and those that draw strictly from divine source. The art of death midwifery falls into the latter. It is my feeling, based on personal experimentation, that channeling energy exclusively from the divine is the most powerful, beneficial, and safest way to work with the light, for both he who serves and he who is served. Using personal energy, in my opinion, depletes the death midwife and dilutes the light being focused on the one served.

This work is also founded upon my more than 30 years of study and work in a professional career as a singer/dancer/actress. It is through the disciplines and techniques used by artists in honing their craft that the spiritual warm-up referred to in this book as "the process" was born.

For those with understanding, life is an art. Death is no less so. It is from that understanding that we offer you *The Art of Death Midwifery.*

AN INVITATION

On Death

You would know the secret of death. But how shall you find it unless you seek it in the heart of life? The owl whose night-bound eyes are blind unto the day cannot unveil the mystery of light. If you would indeed behold the spirit of death, open your heart wide unto the body of life.

For life and death are one, even as the river and the sea are one. In the depth of your hopes and desires lies your silent knowledge of the beyond; And like seeds dreaming beneath the snow your heart dreams of spring. Trust the dreams, for in them is hidden the gate to eternity. Your fear of death is but the trembling of the shepherd when he stands before the king whose hand is to be laid upon him in honour. Is the shepherd not joyful beneath his trembling, that he shall wear the mark of the king?

Yet is he not more mindful of his trembling? For what is it to die but to stand naked in the wind and to melt into the sun? And what is it to cease breathing, but to free the breath from its restless tides, that it may rise and expand and seek God unencumbered? Only when you drink from the river of silence shall you indeed sing. And when you have reached the mountain top, then you shall begin to climb. And when the earth shall claim your limbs, then shall you truly dance.

– Kahlil Gibran

Welcome, friend. You were drawn to pick up this book. Why is that, do you suppose? Have you lost a loved one? Do you fear death? Are you a spiritual adventurer, ever exploring the mystical terrains? Are you one who already serves the dying and wants to go more deeply into this service? Do you feel called? Do you feel the urge to honor, support, and create a sacred space for one of life's most mysterious and transformational transitions? Does that idea inspire you? Or are you just curious?

In any case, you are welcomed here. Have a cup of tea and sit with us a while. We want you to meet our friend, death.

"Death?" you ask. "Death is your friend?"

Don't be afraid. Don't back away. Come. Sit. Watch. Be open. Learn. Remember. Become familiar again with death, and you, too, can become friends. That is the way it used to be long, long ago, beyond memory. Both death and life were our friends back then, and we knew them well. Somewhere along the way, we lost our connection to death. What we once knew and welcomed in its right time, we now fear as a dangerous stranger. It need not be that way. Sit...relax...have a cup of tea and let's get reacquainted. We promise it will be well worth your while.

If you are still reading at this point, it is by no accident. Whether you realize it or not, an invitation has been extended. Something in your life brought you to this place where you are now reading this book about the art of death midwifery and wondering what it is and what it might offer. Something wants you to look into the face of death and know it, remember it, understand it, and perhaps even accept it back into your circle of friends. Something wants you to serve yourself or serve others. The question is, **Will you accept the invitation?**

We hope that you do. We hope you will join us for a while, sit back, and remember together the art of death midwifery.

BIRTH OF A DEATH MIDWIFE

When a baby comes into the world, it emerges from its mother's womb head first. Why is this? You have also noticed that people dive into the water - an element denser than air - head down, but when they come up for air they resurface head up. A baby comes into this world head down because, like the spirit which descends from on high, it plunges into the denser regions of matter. The position of the infant is therefore symbolic: it indicates that the spirit is being engulfed in matter. On the contrary, when a human being dies, he leaves a very dense region and enters a subtler one, like the diver who comes up for air. Birth is therefore a form of death: when a baby is born, it dies in the subtle realms. And when someone dies on earth, he is born on high.

– Omraam Mikhaël Aïvanhov

In 1991 life as I knew it and lived it ended. It happened without warning. Or perhaps, I should say, if there was any warning, I was too steeped in denial to see it. Everything I was, everything I cared about, was striped away, layer by layer, leaving me raw, wounded, and naked. Exposed to the bone and thrown into the bleak black night of the soul, I nearly didn't survive. In fact I did die. I died to all that came before. Slowly, painfully emerging on the other side of this darkness, from the ashes, I was reborn and placed upon a path I could never have imagined - that of a death midwife.

Before 1991, death was a wave whose current grew stronger with AIDS riding its crest. It swept away a huge number of the people I had worked with and cared about in the Broadway theatre arena, where I'd worked for many years as a singer/dancer/actress. Directors, choreographers, composers, lyricists, actors, singers, dancers, friends, and acquaintances were gone in a matter of a few years, cut down in their prime. I mourned and grieved each loss until I thought there were no more tears left in the world. But I was so very wrong.

In February of 1991, my 13-year-old puppy, my Maggie Mae, died. I'd never had a dog live as long as she did. My parents owned a restaurant outside of Chicago and bought the home next door on a major highway. My childhood dogs were no match for that highway, and all died young. My mother, doing her best to "protect" me from death, made up fanciful stories about my dogs running away and being picked up and taken home by loving strangers. I believed her. So Maggie was the first dog I ever had that died of natural causes.

Completely unprepared for Maggie's death, I handled things badly. Since then, wracked with guilt, I've had to face and acknowledge my inadequacy that day. On the day we rushed a very sick Maggie to the vet, we were told she had liver cancer, that she was in renal failure, and that there was nothing he could do. Trying to "protect" me from death, the vet warned me away from being with my Maggie when he administered the shot that would end her suffering. He told me that she might convulse, and it could be a very frightening experience. Fleeing into the night like a coward, I left my baby on that cold metal table to leave this world alone. To this day, I seek forgiveness for abandoning her. I have come to understand that Maggie was my teacher. She loved me unconditionally and made this sacrifice to prepare me for the momentous initiation yet to come.

Six months later, the red light flashed, flashed, flashed a warning on my answering machine. A surreal sense of deja-vu flooded me, and a cold sinking feeling churned in the pit of my stomach as everything went into slow motion. Slowly making my way to the telephone as if underwater, I knew when I touched that red flashing light, my life would irrevocably change. I knew this call was about John.

John was my musical soul mate, virtuoso pianist, and dearest heart friend. For seven years we played the nightclubs in Palm Beach, Florida, and wrote music together. Then suddenly, he disappeared without warning. It had been six weeks with no word. All attempts to find him were futile. Finally, with this phone call, I knew where he was. He was in the ICU of Pontiac, Michigan's General Hospital. Dying.

I'd never been to an ICU before. I stayed away from hospitals altogether, intensely fearing and distrusting the medical field in general; but I was going to be with this person I loved no matter what. I wouldn't let him down as I had Maggie. So, closing out my paltry savings account, I grabbed the next plane out of West Palm Beach to be with him.

Clueless about death, I had no idea what to expect. Like many in western culture, death was not something I thought a great deal about. However, my spiritual teacher at the time, an Indian guru, taught that if we ever had the extreme honor to be in the presence of one who is dying, we should just be a witness and miracles would happen.

Miracles did. I stayed with John during his last four hours on earth. Though he was on a ventilator and unable to speak, we communicated mind- to-mind, heart-to-heart, and soul-to-soul. I heard him clearly inside my head. We'd had the ability to reach into each other's mind in the past so it wasn't too surprising that we did so now. He left without a word because he couldn't tell me he was dying from AIDS. He hinted at it, but I refused to hear. Not him. I couldn't lose him. I told him I wouldn't survive if he died so he stole away like a thief in the night, taking his terrible secret with him.

That afternoon, alone together in the ICU, we had time to say the things we needed to say…to hear the things we needed to hear. In the final hour, a very definite shift began. I could sense John losing consciousness, entering into a coma state. His voice slowly faded from inside my head. The nurses turned off all the alarms while the room grew eerily still. I held his cold, swollen, blue hand. Slowly, the air over his body began circling, gently at first, then swirling and building in velocity. It whirled like a cyclone, so fast my head spun, making me dizzy. I quickly checked the walls to see if they were moving. The room was deathly still, yet the vortex continued over his body, faster and faster, until finally, like water down a drain, the energy suctioned down deep into the center of his body.

I checked the monitors and watched his heart rate and respirations go down...down...down...and eventually flat-line. Alone in the room, I listened to the sush-sushing of the ventilator forcing air into John's lungs. But it was over. He was gone...or so I thought. Holding his cold, swollen, hand, I sat very still and was shocked by what happened next. Literally. All of a sudden, his hand twitched while three very strong electrical shocks jolted me. Then...I felt his spirit detach and begin leaving his body. There is no real way to describe this in words or explain how I knew what was happening. I just... *knew.*

We were still holding hands, so that is where I felt his spirit begin ascending from his body like a hive of bees, thousands of them, buzzing. At the same time, I felt our souls entwined, one inside the other, no boundaries, no me or he, just this commingling of us that was far more intimate than physical intercourse and more ecstatic than any orgasm one might experience in the flesh. I heard him for the last time in this world, inside my head, saying goodbye for now and telling me he loved me, thanking me for being there for him. I don't know how long this moment actually lasted. It happened in that liminal space where time ceases to exist, in a place between worlds. It was the most sensually rich and textured experience of my life, and I knew that I was forever changed by it.

John's spirit continued its ascent and *poof*! He was gone, our connection broken. So was I. Broken, bereft, and so terribly, terribly alone.

In the days and weeks that followed John's death, I nearly drowned in a sea of grief. There was no family support. I was unable to find any support in the community. There was a lot of judgment about people with AIDS back then and very little compassion for the dead or for those who mourned them. Besides, I wasn't even family. There was no blood tie to John. No legal relationship. He was just someone I loved. The message was, "Really, just get on with your life. Get over it!"

Not knowing where to turn or what to do, my soul-agony was unbearable. The suffering almost swept me over the edge and down into the abyss. I teetered for a very long time, so close to letting go and allowing myself to plunge to its depths. Hearing darkness whisper my name, inviting me into its embrace, it was so very tempting to give in, to give up.

At the very last minute, I made a choice to dig in my nails and slowly, painfully drag myself back into the land of the living. I made a choice to survive this horrific loss, which not only took one of the most important people in my life, but also took my identity, my career, and all my social connections. Everything that I valued in life died with John.

Slowly, when I was finally able to put coherent sentences together, I started learning everything I could about death, dying, the afterlife, grief, mourning, loss, and consciousness. As I grew stronger, I began to work in the field of death and dying with AIDS organizations, hospices, and home health care companies around the country. I companioned the dying and provided physical care in both paid and volunteer positions. In the back of my mind was the knowing that what I experienced with

John, that communion that existed beyond words, in that liminal space, could be duplicated. I just wasn't sure how. Not yet.

When my parents approached death, I changed my life in order to be with them in the final weeks and months, to help them each have the best possible transition I could offer. With my mother's death in 2003, a shift began, taking my work to an even deeper level. I realized that I needed to do deep spiritual work, healing the wounds, and cleansing the mind, spirit, and body, if I wanted to serve the dying more profoundly. After several years of intense study, I became an interfaith minister with a Doctorate of Divinity in death, dying, and afterlife communications. Those years of meditation and spiritual practice brought me in contact with my team of non-physical, angelic guidance and wisdom, whose on-the-job instruction took my work with the dying deeper and deeper still.

Then in a serendipitous series of events, the palliative care unit of Norfolk General Hospital in Norfolk, VA, asked me to volunteer my services. It is there that all of my various skills and experiences came together to fully walk the path that had begun so long ago on that very sad day in Pontiac General Hospital. With guidance from my team, I began to replicate that deep communication beyond words with the dying that happened spontaneously with John. A teachable discipline and practice took form.

In 2007, after 16 years of ongoing study and practice in the field of death and dying, a new phase of this work unfolded. It was time to share with others what I discovered about communing with the dying. I began offering workshops on the art of death midwifery, and the great interest in them is most heartening. This book is the next step in offering those who feel drawn to this work a more sacred, profound, and meaningful way to serve the dying.

What is the Art of Death Midwifery?

The art of death midwifery is a profound and intuitive way of communing with the dying, of lending support and guidance to those making this greatest of transitions. Committing to deep spiritual work, the death midwife becomes a strong, clear conduit who directs the flow of divine love to the dying. Death midwifery is a spiritual art that creates a sacred space using music, voice, meditation, guided imagery, and inspiration. Most importantly, the death midwife gives sustained, unconditionally loving attention to the dying with the intention that divine right action in divine right timing inform the process.

The bond between the death midwife and the one served is sacrosanct. Such extreme intimacy requires time for a deep level of trust to develop. It is an honor and a privilege to be allowed to commune with one during this most awe-inspiring of transformations, and this honor should never be taken lightly.

Through continued practice, the death midwife learns to navigate smoothly through various levels of consciousness in order to meet and match the consciousness of the one served. Having made this link, the death midwife can literally swim in her charge's stream of consciousness and commune at the most subtle of levels, even with those deemed "unresponsive" by medical standards.

In many ancient and indigenous cultures, there were those charged with assisting the dying. These were often shamans or persons of spiritual power who acted as guides or psychopomps for those crossing over. The Nanai shamans of the Russian far east[1], the death houses of ancient China[2] and the Tibetans with their landmark guide for the dying known as The Tibetan Book of the Dead all served this function.

In mythology, Egyptian gods of the underworld Osiris and Anubis, as well as Hermes, son of Zeus and the Greek goddess Hecate, were guides of the dying. In ancient Brittany there was Ankou; for the Gauls of ancient Italy and France there was Epona. Freyja and the Valkyries guided ancient Norse souls to the afterlife. These cultures and others understood the need of the dying for support, not only on this shore of the physical, but also while crossing the river and finding one's footing on the shore of the non-physical.

Modern western culture has all but forgotten this soul need. Very often this most sacred of journeys, this adventure, which should be filled with reverence, mystery, and awe, is instead fraught with fear, turmoil, and anguish. Our ignorance, often disguised as sophistication, has turned dying from a transition into the fullness of our eternal being into a failure and a tragedy. It does not need to be this way.

---

1 Native Peoples of Russia's Maritime Province, ©Edward J. Vajda, West Washington University

2 www.pilgrimshospice.ca

Slowly, people are re-awakening. We realize that somehow we are misunderstanding something important about the great mystery called death. Slowly, people are beginning to want more for both themselves and their loved ones at this most sacred of times.

Baby Boomers, that demographic juggernaut of a catalyst, are becoming senior citizens. Just as they have made their mark on every other phase of life they've entered, they will also re-define our death experience. This is the generation that will embrace the revival of the death midwife.

The 21st century death midwife is part mystic, part shaman, part artist. Rather than healers per se, death midwives are gatekeepers to the realms of spirit and guides to the "other world." The choice of the term "midwife" is clear: We assist and guide the dying into the birth of a new life. We recognize and honor the understanding that death is not an ending but a transition into a different frequency of existence—an existence that, while different, is nevertheless as real as the one we are in now.

A death midwife guides and supports the transitioning from this life into the next. The focus remains on the person dying, not on the family. At the same time, we understand and respect the sorrow of those left behind to mourn this ultimate change of relationship. We understand that this relationship continues, but now in a new form. Once the transition is made, we then support those left behind to mourn fully and freely and, in time, to integrate their loss.

In the future, it is my hope that professional death midwives will be an integral part of palliative care units in hospitals, hospices, and nursing homes. Lay death midwives will care for their family and loved ones at home. As the work we do is on an energetic and spiritual level, we are neither health care professionals nor chaplains; yet we bridge an important gap in both. We do what the doctors, nurses, and chaplains cannot do: We remain present with our patients physically, mentally, emotionally, and spiritually for long periods of time. We companion the dying, holding vigil when no one else can or will. For the dying, just knowing that they are safe, that they are surrounded by love, and that they are never alone is often the greatest gift we give.

It is extremely helpful to have a guide outside the family dynamic to create and hold this sacred space. Often the tremendous feelings of loss, fear, anxiety, and regret make it nearly impossible for those closest to the one dying to create and maintain that sacred space for their loved one. This is perfectly understandable, perfectly human. The death midwife fills that role, allowing family, friends, and loved ones to do the difficult grief work they need to do while he maintains undivided loving attention upon the dying.

The art of death midwifery honors all spiritual traditions and philosophies. It is a deeply spiritual calling that embraces the mystical teachings of Judaism, Christianity, Islam, Buddhism, Hinduism, Zen, Tao, Paganism, Wicca, Shamanism, etc. At all times it respects the belief system of the one dying. It is not our purpose to save souls but rather to honor souls in their journey to new life.

The art of death midwifery has no agenda other than to be of service. It draws from ancient traditions, while at the same time it's new and foreign to current western cultures. It is about love, about loving others as we hope to be loved ourselves. It is a gift offered with no thought of reward. It is the gift of being present, sometimes to unbearable suffering, to be willing to create and hold sacred space so that the one dying will feel safe to engage in the great labor that being born into a new life requires.

At the funeral service for a young woman I had the honor of serving, the minister spoke of Mary Magdalene. He told of how Mary stayed with Jesus as he was crucified, watched him suffer, stayed with him as he died. "Mary loved Jesus enough to watch him die," he said. That's what death midwives do; we love people enough to watch them die.

Who Can Practice the Art of Death Midwifery?

The art of death midwifery can be learned and practiced to a degree by anyone with a deep, abiding desire to serve the dying. I say to a degree because you can only go as deeply as you are willing to plumb inner depths and do the required work. I invite you to be open and willing. To be, as my spiritual teacher and mentor suggests, a "spiritual scientist" and to experiment with the discipline and techniques presented in The Art of Death Midwifery.

This path of service can be practiced by doctors, nurses, social workers, massage therapists, chaplains, hospice personnel and volunteers, family members, and friends. It can be used for patients, clients, family, friends, loved ones, and pets. Old and young will benefit. What I find in my workshops is that perhaps the one most profoundly affected by this work will be you.

Time and time again I hear from our workshop participants how "life-altering" this work is. I certainly know this is true from my own experience, but it is continually confirmed by the feedback I get from students. You cannot be open to this work and not be deeply affected by it.

Not only can you use the art of death midwifery to birth yourself into life in the non-physical realms, but, through the act of committing to this work, to this path of service, you will give birth to a new you in *this* life.

You cannot travel the terrain of various levels of consciousness and not see things differently. You cannot be present in the face of tremendous suffering and not know grace. You cannot look into the face of death, your own and others', and not be reborn. You cannot give without thought of reward and not be given a thousand times more in return.

The art of death midwifery is for anyone with the strength and courage to look inside where all our fears of death, both personal and cultural, are hidden and to restore them to the light.

If you are reading this far, the Art of Death Midwifery might be for **you.**

DEATH AS AN INITIATION

"Death is a friend of ours; and he that is not ready to entertain him is not at home."

– Sir Francis Bacon

It is my belief that no one consciously *chooses* to become a death midwife. This path chooses *you.* Though many may travel this path in part, it truly is not for everyone, nor should it be. One cannot be forced to this path. It will call to you, perhaps quietly at first, but becoming evermore insistent until you pay heed. Doors to other paths will close along the way until finally, only this path is clear and you *know* without question that you are meant to do this work. You will find that as you surrender to this calling, miraculous synchronicities will conspire to aid you. Things will "click" into place and doors will open. You need only the courage to walk through the open door and be willing to travel the path. If you do, you will find that you are never alone. You will always be provided with the help that you need if your heart and intentions are pure. That intention is simply to serve.

To be initiated onto this path of service we must be bloodied by grief. We need to be broken open and rubbed raw by the death of a beloved...a parent, a spouse, a lover, a friend, a sibling, or a pet. We need to be brought to our knees by grief and travel to the very depths of despair. Before initiation is offered we need to teeter over the precipice of our beliefs about death and about life. It is in the shadow world, the deepest depths, the dark-of-the-moon phase of life, the dark night of the soul, when we are cracked open and bleeding, when we are at our most vulnerable from the agony of loss, that the opportunity is present.

It is when are we are faced with the inescapability of death that we are pushed to the very limits of our beliefs. It is quite easy to contemplate death from the safety of youth and good health. It is easy to delude ourselves with notions of our physical immortality. It is easy to deny death in a culture that supports us in this at every turn; a culture that views death as an enemy, as a failure; a culture that values youth and beauty while disrespecting age and experience; a culture that shuns the dying and those who mourn them. When imminent death is in your face, when your death or the death of one you love is approaching, what ***now*** do you believe? What do you really think about death? About the afterlife? About life and what you value most in it?

It is in living through this experience that initiation may be offered. No amount of intellectual knowledge, no titles or degrees, will bring you to this point. Only your soul, willing to immolate and trusting that the hand of the God of your understanding is there to pull you from the flames, will open the door to a new life.

Sounds fun, huh? Well, consider this. While we cannot control the manner of death, ours or another's, *we can choose how we experience death.* We can experience death as either a tragedy or a bittersweet opportunity for transformation. We do not disregard or deny the sadness of parting, but instead use it to transmute our pain into grace.

I promise if you surrender to the fire of this initiation, if you allow it to burn away your fears and anxieties, your misconceptions about life and death…you may be reborn and find yourself on the path of service I call the art of death midwifery.

SACRED MAGIC

Sacred magic is the power behind the art of death midwifery. Hermeticism, which is a set of philosophical beliefs based primarily upon the writings attributed to Hermes Trismegistus, defines sacred magic as the science of love.[3] For some, the word magic might be uncomfortable so the term divine science can be substituted. In this book, however, we will use the term sacred magic. By magic we mean the unseen and spiritual beyond and beneath the seen and material. Love is the element that gives sacred magic its potency.

To illustrate an example of sacred magic we will use a story from the Bible about the disciple Peter:

"Now as Peter went here and there among them all, he came down also to the saints that lived at Lydda. There he found a man named Aeneas, who had been bedridden for eight years and was paralyzed. And Peter said to him: Aeneas, Jesus Christ heals you; rise and make your bed. And immediately he rose." (Acts *ix*, 32-34)

This story demonstrates for us the three key elements of Sacred Magic and legitimizes its use:

1. From a moral standpoint it is an act of pure charity.

2. From a spiritual standpoint the healing comes from a divine source.

---

3 Anonymous. (2002) *Meditations on the Tarot; A Journey into Christian Hermeticism.* New York, NY; Jeremy P. Tarcher/Penguin, pg. 55.

3. From a physical standpoint the healing is perfect to the individual.[4]

In this example we see that Peter had no intention other than to be of service to Aeneas. The healing does not originate from Peter but rather from the divine. Finally, the healing is exactly what Aeneas needed.

In respect to the art of death midwifery, it is important that we remember that *we* are not healers. We are guides and conduits. Through aligning our will with divine will, divine healing may flow, but that healing, being perfect to the individual, can take many forms. Very often in our case, that form will be a more sacred, reverent death and not a return to good health.

Though Peter is not the healer, *Peter is essential to the process.* His presence and voice are needed for this divine transmission to flow. This act, being an act of love, requires the perfect union of divine will and human will. This act serves both the divine and man. This is the power of true service and is the legitimacy of sacred magic.

We as death midwives, serve as the last link in a magical chain that descends from above. We serve as an earthly *point of contact and point of concentration* for the operation created, willed, and initiated from above. Sacred magic's ultimate mantra is: **May that which is above *be* as that which is below; and may that which is below *be* as that which is above.**[5]

---

4 Ibid.

5 Ibid, pg. 56-57.

There is an order to sacred magic for it to flow:

1. True contact with the divine.

2. Taking into consciousness this true contact.

3. Putting into effect the inspiration given.[6]

What does all this mean? First it means committing to the great and often difficult inner work necessary to develop the discernment to recognize real and true contact with the God of your understanding. This comes with prayer and meditation. It is in prayer and meditation that we begin strengthening our spiritual muscles. This is where we become flexible, sensitive, and responsive to the unseen world. Through prayer and meditation we draw the divine and all its helpers closer to us, establishing a true relationship. With practice, we learn to sort astral fantasies from spiritual reality. It takes time and dedication to grow familiar with the terrain of the spirit, but it is absolutely essential to the work. Just as we wouldn't set out on a long journey without a map, neither does it make sense to travel the inner terrains without learning the landscape of the spirit world.

Once we are able to make this true connection and become familiar with the terrain, *we must have faith that we have done so.* We must trust in this connection. Trust, too, comes with time as we deepen our relationship to the Source until we *know* it is so.

---

6 Ibid, pg. 58

Finally, we must put into practice the inspiration we receive. This is why it is so important in practicing the art of death midwifery to be firmly connected to our higher power and to be certain of that connection. Before acting upon an inspiration we must be sure that inspiration is from a divine source and not from our own ego. As we begin practicing the art of death midwifery, it is better to simply witness inspiration as it arises without acting on it. As we grow more skilled in the practice, as we strengthen our connection to the Source and can be certain of its origin, then action becomes appropriate.

The aim of sacred magic is to restore freedom to those who have lost it. As their body's functions slowly fade, the dying are very often steeped in feelings of powerlessness. The art of death midwifery seeks to alleviate the fear, anxiety, isolation, and sense of separation so often experienced by the dying. It seeks to empower by creating and holding the sacred space necessary for the labor required to transition into a new life with grace and dignity.

Sacred magic is *never* forced upon the one served. It is a gift freely given. Purity of will is its potency. The goal is to establish freedom of choice through the knowing of truth. Truth does not struggle against the false, it merely *is*. As death midwives we create and hold the space of knowing that life is eternal, that consciousness continues, and that death is not an end but a transition into new life, whatever that may be. We hold that space of knowing regardless of the anguish or suffering those we serve may be experiencing, but we **do not force, nor do we have the**

power to force, that knowing. We do, however, remain containers for that knowing.

The art of death midwifery is a gift offered to those we love enough to watch them die. It is a gift that can be accepted or denied. Most often it is accepted, but not always. We must understand clearly that we **have no power to force its acceptance.** The free will with which we are all endowed **cannot** be violated. **To think we have the power to overrule another's free will is delusion, and we will pay a price for that arrogance.**

The practice of sacred magic involves taking on the infirmities of others.[7] In Galatians *vi,* 2 Paul enjoins us to "Bear one another's burdens and so fulfill the law of Christ." This is the way the saints practiced sacred magic, not by infusing someone with their own personal energy, but by taking from him what was unhealthy. It is extremely important to note that in practicing the art of death midwifery we may employ various techniques to draw off pain and suffering, but we ***do not*** take that pain and suffering *into* ourselves. Instead, we draw it off and offer it to Gaia, to Mother Earth, asking her to recycle, restore, and return that energy to its highest expression. We will explore that practice in the "Techniques" section of the book.

Far more important than any technique, however, is the ability and willingness to bear another's burden. This is probably the most valuable and difficult gift we offer. To be in the presence of another's great suffering, to bear the burden of her anguish, while continuing to hold

7 Ibid. pg. 62.

that space in the face of unbearable sorrow, is the ultimate test we as death midwives will face. Here in western culture we want to *fix* things. We want to make it better. If the gift of the art of death midwifery is accepted, if sacred magic flows, things may change for the better. There are times, however, when all we can offer is our presence to bear witness and keep sacred space open in the face of physical, mental, emotional, and/or spiritual agony. We will address this more in the "Bearing Witness in the Garden of Gethsemane" section.

While the role of sacred magic in the art of death midwifery is crucial, we must always remember that, in our practice, the "healing" that takes place will most likely be a more conscious and transformative death. That is a priceless gift.

MYTHOLOGY OF THE DEATH GUIDE

The gods conceal from men the happiness of death, that they may endure life.

– Lucan

Included in many religious belief systems is the concept of death guides, also known as psychopomps. It is the sacred charge of these individuals, whether they be angels, spirits, deities, humans, or animals, to guide the dying and newly dead into the afterlife. The word psychopomp comes from the Greek *ψυχοπομπός*, psyche (soul, spirit, or mind) and pompos (guide). In most cases, These spirit guides do not judge the dying. Their sacred responisibility is to lead the dying and the newly dead safely to the farther shore.

These guides are found in the mythology of most cultures including African, Celtic, Christian, Egyptian, Etruscan, Greek, Hindu, Inuit, Islamic, Judaic, Mayan, Native American, Norse, Persian, Polynesian, Roman, Slavic, Vodun, and Zoroastrian. While it is beyond the scope of this book to delve deeply into this phenomenon, it is worth noting a few of these death guides.

In the Christian tradition, Archangel Michael is given the office of rescuing "the souls of the faithful from the power of the enemy, especially at the hour of death."[8]

8 The Catholic Encyclopedia, Volume X. Published 1911. New York: Robert Appleton Company. Nihil Obstat, October 1, 1911. Remy Lafort, S.T.D., Censor. Imprimatur. +John Cardinal Farley, Archbishop of New York

St. Peter is the keeper of the keys of the Kingdom of Heaven.

The ancient Egyptians worshiped Anubis, the jackal-headed god. He was a god of the afterlife, "He who stands upon His mountain," protector of the deceased. It was Anubis in the Egyptian Book of the Dead who weighed the heart of the newly deceased against the weight of a feather to determine the worthiness of that individual to enter the Underworld. He is considered the gatekeeper and ruler of the Underworld, the protector of those souls journeying there. Guardian of the veil, he is the god of dying more than the god of death.

In ancient Greek mythology, there are Hermes (who is also Mercury in Roman Mythology) and Hekate. Hermes was the Olympian god of boundaries and those who cross them. He was an escort for the dead, helping them to find their way to the afterlife, and along with Hekate, was one of the few gods who could safely travel the Underworld.

Hekate, thought originally to be a Thracian goddess, but adopted by both the Greeks and Romans, is midwife to the souls of the dying. A liminal goddess of the crossways, she governs the borders between the physical world and the spiritual world.

The Hindus have Pushan, the god of meeting. Responsible for journeys, he also serves as a guide to the souls of the dying, protecting and supporting while conducting them to the other world. The Islamic tradition honors the archangel of death, Azrael. His names means "whom God helps."[9] In mystic Judaism, the cabalists believe that archangel Sandalphon stands at the crossroads of Paradise and leads the righteous to Heaven.

In Norse mythology, the female deities known as the Valkyries carried the most heroic who died in battle to Valhalla. The Celts believed that Epona and her horses led the dead in the afterlife ride.[10] In many cultures, animals, such as eagles, owls, ravens, butterflies, dogs, horses, and dolphins, also serve as guides to the otherworlds.[11]

Though Native American tribal customs vary in expression, they agree that life is a circle into death and again into rebirth.[12] In Cahuilla Indian culture, Muut was the personification of death and usually took the form of an owl that led the dying to new life.[13]

Most often, indigenous cultures turn to their shaman. This man or woman is often the tribal spiritual leader who, through an ecstatic state with the transcendent world, is permitted to escort the dead to the otherworlds. Through years of arduous study, shamans become adept at traveling through various altered states of consciousness, bridging ordinary and non-ordinary realms of existence. Assisting in the transition between life and death, they assure the survival of the soul after the physical body

---

9 Davidson, Gustav (1967), *A Dictionary of Angels, Including The Fallen Angels*, Entry: **Azrael**, pp. 64, 65, Library of Congress Catalog Card Number: 66-19757

10 Hubert, "Le mythe d'Epona" *Mélanges linguistiques offerts à M. J.Vendryes* (1925) pp 187-198

11 Laura Strong, Ph.D., psychopomps.org

12 Blair A. Moffett. Sunrise magazine, November 1980. Copyright © 1980 by Theosophical University Press

13 Ryan Tuccinardi (1998), MMVI Encyclopedia Mythica Online

has served its purpose.[14] One example of this shamanic practice is the weeping woman of the arctic region, whose vocalizations called the souls of the dying to the other shore.[15]

Even this brief summary of death guides could not fail to pay honor to the Tibetan culture. The Tibetan Book of the Dead, or Bardo Thodol, may be the preeminent manual for the journey we call death. Dating back to the 8th century, the book is a guide for souls traveling from the moment of death to rebirth. In this belief system when the soul is freed from the body it creates a new reality, much like a dream. These different dreams or bardos can be both magnificent and terrifying. Since initially there is confusion, when the soul finds itself without a body it needs reassurance and guidance so that it can attain enlightenment or nirvana. The Tibetan culture, steeped in reverence for the mysteries of death, has practiced an ancient form of death midwifery for centuries.

These examples indicate that from time immemorial there have been those who served the dying as companions and guides to the next world. It is only in the more recent past that we have lost our guidance. With the advent of modern medicine, death and dying ceased being a rite to be honored as a natural part of the cycle of life and instead became an enemy to be defeated. We deny death and shun the dying, often packing them off to nursing homes or hospitals to make their transition alone in-

---

14 Krippner, Stanley, *Shamans as Mythmakers and Psychopomps,* Articles Online, Centro de Estudios Oníricos de Chile.

15 Encyclopædia Britannica. 2008. Encyclopædia Britannica Online.

stead of being at home surrounded by their loved ones. We shelter our young from death until we now have a culture that seems to believe death is an option rather than an inevitability. We invent ways to look to the farthest reaches of the universe yet fear looking into the face of the dying. Facing death without fear may truly be the final frontier.

Now we have the baby-boomers heading into our senior years. Just as we have re-defined our generation's values concerning so many things, we will re-define how we wish to experience the final transition in our lives. Many of us will desire a more supportive, sacred, loving, and transformational birth into new life. We will want the companionship and aide of a spiritual death midwife available to us. The time has come to welcome back the psychopomp as a valued member of society.

THE SCIENCE BENEATH THE ART

If the doors of perception were cleansed, everything would appear to man as it is, infinite.

– William Blake

Spiritual death midwifery is and will forever remain an art. However, as our understanding of quantum physics becomes more advanced, we begin to see some interesting principles that may underlie and support our work as death midwives. Though I have no claims to being any kind of scientist other than a spiritual scientist, I'd like to share some thoughts for you to ponder as you explore the path of death midwifery.

The observational theory of the early 1970s, which in accordance with the work of Nobel laureates John Eccles and Eugene Wigner, as well as neuroscientist Wilder Penfield and mathematician John von Neumann, suggests a symmetry of physics: "…that the action of matter upon mind must give rise to… a 'direct action of mind upon matter.' "[16]

In support of that contention, physicist Bernard d'Espagnat states, "The doctrine that the world is made up of objects whose existence is independent of human

16 Radin, D. (2006). *Entangled Minds.* New York, NY: Paraview Pocket Books, pg. 251.

consciousness turns out to be in conflict with quantum mechanics and with facts established by experiment."[17]

Now consider the concept of the zero point field, first proposed by Albert Einstein and Otto Stern in 1913. It is defined as an all-inclusive "field of fields" that encompasses every unseen particle in the universe. Calculated to contain 10 to the 40th power more energy than the known universe, the unseen becomes more powerful than the seen.[18] This may be the same field called the collective unconscious by psychiatrist Carl Jung, the morphogenetic field by biologist Rupert Sheldrake, and the Akasha by the Vedic tradition of Hinduism. These various theories postulate the existence of a non-local memory permeating time and space with which we can each resonate. If any of these theories prove true, we then may have a foundation for the premise that, by our focused and loving attention, we can connect with those dying at deep core levels and positively affect the journey they are taking.

In addition, the work of Dean Radin, PhD, laboratory director for the Institute of Noetic Sciences, on the entangled mind theory is quite compelling. According to Radin, Erwin Schrödinger, who won the Nobel Prize in physics in 1933, referred to entanglement as "connections between separated particles that persist regardless of distance." The connections are instantaneous and operating outside the usual flow of time. Schrödinger sug-

17 d'Espagnat, B. (November 1979). The quantum theory and reality. *Scientific American*, 158-181.

18 Chopra, D. (2006). *Life After Death*. New York, NY: Harmony Books, pg. 199-200.

gested that physical reality is connected in ways we are just beginning to understand.[19]

Physicists speculate that entanglement extends to everything in the universe initiating from the Big Bang; therefore everything is already entangled. Contemplate the idea that our minds might be entangled with the universe or as Schrödinger contends, "Hence this life of yours which you are living, is not merely a piece of the entire existence, but is, in a certain sense, the whole; only this whole is not so constituted that it can be surveyedin a single glance." Is it possible we might be living within a holistic, deeply inter-connected reality? Might we, in fact, at the deepest level, all b*e* one?[20]

Or imagine the universe as a giant bowl of clear jello with every wiggle being felt throughout the entirety? Through each jiggle we can get glimpses of other people's minds—not through the ordinary senses but because, at some level, our minds already coexist with every other mind and everything else. To navigate through this "jello," we use attention and intention.[21]

Now lets add to all the above the observer effect proposed in the 1970s, which refers to the changes that the act of observing will have on the phenomenon observed. One theory suggests that the act of observation literally creates physical reality. While this is still a controversial theory within physics, Nobel Laureate physicists Eugene Wigner and Brian Josephson, John Wheeler, and John

---

19 Radin, D. (2006.) *Entangled Minds*. New York, NY: Paraview Pocket Books, pg. 260-266.

20 Ibid.

21 Ibid.

von Neumann have embraced concepts at least mildly sympathetic to this view.[22] Regarding the art of death midwifery, meditate upon the proposition that by our focused attention on the one we serve, we do indeed affect change.

Next, there is the work of Julian Jaynes, PhD in psychology from Yale. In The Origin of Consciousness in the Breakdown of the Bicameral Mind he presents the theory that until about three thousand years ago, humans were in a constant state of "hallucination" that allowed speaking with the spirit world. (Notice the bias in the use of the word "hallucination." I suggest it may not have been hallucination at all.) In other words, until 3000 years ago, humans had only the subconscious mind to encounter and communicate with the world. The conscious mind had not yet developed. Therefore rather than "hallucinating," it might be said that they had direct communication with the unseen world. If this is true, then with the art of death midwifery we are, in some ways, reawakening and revitalizing that mode of consciousness.

Finally, I'd like to mention the intention experiments of Gary Schwartz and Lynne McTaggart. In her book, The Intention Experiment, Lynne McTaggart posits that through the quantum nature of thoughts and intention, humans are both receivers and transmitters of quantum signals. The result of these experiments suggest that directed intention appears to manifest as both electrical and magnetic energy and produce an ordered stream of photons *visible and measurable* by sensitive equipment.

22 Ibid, pg. 251.

Lynne asserts that, "We must open our minds to the wisdom of many native traditions, which hold an intuitive understanding of intention. Virtually all these cultures describe a unified energy field not unlike the zero point field, holding everything in the universe in its invisible web. These other cultures understand our place in the hierarchy of energy and the value of choosing time and place with care. The modern science of remote influence has finally offered proof of ancient intuitive beliefs about manifestation, healing, and the power of thoughts. We would do well to appreciate, as these traditional cultures do, that every thought is sacred, with the power to take physical form."[23]

If we consider all of these fascinating theories together, we might extrapolate from them that:

By the act of our focused loving presence, combined with our intention to be clear strong conduits for directing divine energy, we can effect a change in the one we serve, facilitating that person's transition from his or her physical form into his or her non-physical form with greater ease, peace, dignity, respect, and even joy.

While having a foundation of scientific principle that might support us in our work is comforting, it must be remembered that death midwifery is, at its roots, an art just as medicine once was, and in its highest form, re-

23 McTaggart, L. (2007). *The Intention Experiment.* New York, NY: Simon & Shuster, Inc., pg. 195.

mains. In the art of death midwifery, we may serve as a link between science and imagination, between the seen and unseen worlds. With our palette of skills, we paint a magical bridge from this world to the next for the one we companion to cross. As death midwives we artfully serve as an instrument of the divine, through which plays the alluring nocturne of eternity.

Attributes of a Death Midwife – The Importance of Humility

Compassion, empathy, sensitivity, flexibility, imagination and creativity are the basic tools of the spiritual death midwife. Concentration, focus, and intuition are skills we must cultivate. We are servants to God and to our brothers and sisters who are making this momentous transition, so purity, humility, integrity, and honor must be continually integrated into our being.

Each of us will have our own unique talents that we bring to the practice of the art of death midwifery. Some may be skilled in Reiki or other modes of energy work; some may work with healing touch; some may be medical or spiritual intuitives; others may be musicians or singers, counselors, social workers, nurses, massage therapists, hypnotherapists, or ministers. Any and all of these talents can be used in our work, but always, always remember, this work is not about us. We do not use any of our skills from our ego's need to "do" something. We are merely conduits for Source energy. Of ourselves, we do nothing. We wait upon divine guidance in the application of our gifts. Unlike the doting aunt foisting those fluffy bunny slippers upon us regardless of our actual need or desire, our gifts are offered freely but judiciously…as guided by spirit or our higher self, not as the personal ego wills.

The art of death midwifery is an art of ***being,*** not of ***doing.*** That can be the most difficult aspect of this work, especially for those of us brought up in a western culture that prizes dynamic action. It is natural in the presence of sometimes unbearable suffering to want to initiate action, to *fix* things. We want to make it better, to make it go away. We want to take away all the pain and sorrow, to somehow escape death. There are times when death may and can be postponed, but it is never escaped. If we were able to pierce the veil of death and know its true face, we would not want to escape it. Death is not the enemy. Much of the pain and sorrow of death comes from misunderstanding this mysterious and "awe-full" transformation. Just as in birth, where being prepared helps the laboring mother to relax more into the often painful and frightening experience…so does preparing consciously for death help us to birth ourselves into new life with more ease.

By *being* spiritually centered and balanced, by *being* strong and resilient conduits for divine light, by *being* a focused presence of unconditional love and acceptance, by *being* open and responsive to divine inspiration, by *being* aware of the subtle but direct communication with the dying, the death midwife can create and offer sacred space as a gift to the one he serves. It bears repeating that never does he have the power to force the acceptance of his gift. Everyone at all times has free will. The dying do not relinquish that because they are dying. It isn't even a matter of honoring the dying's wishes. We must understand fully that we, as death midwives, **do not have the**

power to do otherwise. To entertain the thought is hubris and we will dearly pay the price for it.

Humility then, is our constant guide. Trust me, if it is not, the dying will make it so. Many years ago, when I first began companioning the dying, I had a patient who lived out in the desert of Arizona. A widower alone and dying of lung cancer, he kept all his windows darkened with thick curtains. His death was quickly approaching. He had not been "responsive" in several days. I wanted so much to help him. I felt so compelled to do something. So I told him to "go into the light." In the faintest, nearly inaudible whisper, I heard him say to me, "F**k off!" I was stunned! That couldn't be what he just said to me after being "unresponsive" for so long. So I once again told him to "go into the light." Plain as day this time, I heard him say, "F**K off!" Well, let me tell you, I was speechless; and that, dear readers, is what I should have been in the first place. I found out later from his friends that he had suffered from terrible migraines most of his life. Bright lights hurt his eyes terribly. So encouraging this man to "go into the light," no matter how good my intentions, was the worst possible thing I could have done.

My mistake was twofold. First, feeling the need to *do* something from my own personal ego, I did something totally inappropriate for this man. Secondly, I actually thought I had the power to make him go into the light. I didn't. Only he did....and in this case, it wasn't the right thing for him to do. It wasn't the right way for him to make his transition. Please, dear readers, learn from my mistake and do not offend the dying!

If we are not sure that what we are inspired to do or say flows from a divine source, it is better to just *be* and not *do* anything. In sacred magic this corresponds with taking the vows of obedience, poverty, and chastity, not in the literal sense but in the spiritual sense. We sacrifice our will (obedience), thought (poverty) and imagination (chastity) to the God of our understanding that they become instruments of the divine rather than expressions of our small and arbitrary selves.

In order to be vibrant death midwives, we must be able to make quick and intimate connections with the ones we serve. The connection between the death midwife and her charge is one that, due to circumstances within hospitals or nursing homes, often needs to be established quickly. The dying must have great trust in the midwife in order for divine light to flow unimpeded. As we die, our subtle and denser bodies become gradually more permeable while our boundaries slowly soften and dissolve. This aids us greatly in making that connection.

It is important, however, that the energy and manner of the death midwife engender the highest vibrations of trustworthiness and safety. As guides of the souls of the dying we are being granted a tremendous honor. We are allowed to bear witness to another's transformation into a different dimension of life. The bond we create is as sacred and intimate as that between mother and child. Therefore, a death midwife must be comfortable becoming one with another human being at the soul level. It is not work for those who fear intimacy and vulnerability. At the same time, we must always remember that we are guests of this soul and act with the utmost of respect for their invitation to meld.

It might be easy to spin romantic notions of what a deathbed vigil might be or what life as a death midwife is like, but we must guard against this tendency. To *be* a death midwife requires being able to be present to all of death's faces, the light and the dark. That means sometimes being with great pain, suffering, and sorrow. Sometimes the greatest gift we give to those we serve is being able to be present *knowing* that we cannot fix anything and not running away, denying, or condemning, but accepting what is so and being able to bear what is so with the one we serve. That takes great inner strength, which can only be built up with practice. Death can sometimes be messy and smelly and exhausting…just like birth… just like life. We must grow comfortable with death in all of its wonder and mystery and pain and awe-fullness.

As difficult as this may seem, it is possible to see great beauty and grace even in the midst of tremendous travail. When we see with the eyes of the spirit, even in the greatest of sorrow there can be joy. Our challenge is to contain both. Our grace is to be able to contain both.

We are the Instrument – Self Preparation for Working with the Dying

When we work with the dying we step into a different world; we enter a different level of consciousness. It might be more accurate to say that we move between various states of consciousness depending on where the one dying is at the moment. We want to be able to move fluidly from one state to another like a dancer flowing through choreography or a singer effortlessly changing keys during a song. As death midwives, we enter a sacred duet with the one dying. It's a duet performed with reverence and respect. Your partner, the one who is dying, must be able to trust you just as a ballerina trusts her partner not to drop her or as a singer trusts her pianist to accompany her with great finesse and nuance. As with a dancer or a singer, what appears to the onlooker as effortless is, in fact, the result of much preparation and discipline.

We who are drawn to the life path of death midwifery are travelers of the spiritual highways. It matters not which road we choose for that journey but only that our feet are firmly planted in the direction of ever-expanding consciousness. This transition from the physical world to the non-physical world is a mysterious and sacred one. Those who choose to companion others through this transition need to have a spiritually-elevating and consciousness-expanding practice firmly in place. The requirement for on-going spiritual development cannot be stressed enough. The sensitivities and skills required of a death midwife will grow as our practice deepens. It is like playing an instrument: We must first master technique, practicing the scales daily, before approaching the rigors of a Rachmaninoff concerto or a jazz etude. Our spiritual practice tunes our instrument for this work with the intention of making of us clear and pure conduits for divine energy.

Whether one follows a Christian path, a Buddhist path, an Islamic path, a Jewish path, a Pagan path, or a spiritual path of one's own making makes no difference, though a willingness to be open to the mystical elements of the chosen path will stand one in good stead.

Remember that **imagination is the key that unlocks the door to the otherworlds**. All work on the spiritual plane depends on our ability to imagine. That is a beginning step on the path. We need to be willing to allow our imagination to open up our inner senses—our inner sight, inner hearing, inner touch, and inner knowing. Through our willingness to imagine, combined with properly focused discernment, we will come to inner *knowing*...and then imagination will no longer be needed.

SETTING THE STAGE – ESTABLISHING A SPIRITUAL SANCTUARY

Setting the stage by establishing a spiritual sanctuary is a powerful signal to our psyche, to the God of our understanding, and to our spiritual helpers that we are serious about this inner work. A separate room dedicated exclusively to spiritual practice is ideal. If this is not possible, designating a special corner of a room exclusively to spiritual practice will suffice. It is important to do your spiritual practice in the same place so the vibration of the work you do will build up over time. It is also good to do your practice at basically the same time of day, morning, afternoon or night, whatever is most potent for you. This trains the body and mind to move into the required altered states with more ease.

Begin by creating an altar. This can be a small table or nightstand. Design the altar to reflect and support your individual connection with God. Decorate it with beautifully colored silk scarves or whatever feels right. Add pictures and statues of pertinent deities if that resonates. Fresh flowers or other elements of nature may be used.

The ritual of lighting candles and incense sends a signal to the mind that we are beginning our alignment with the divine. Using essential oils conducive to meditation, such as sandalwood, amber, frankincense, myrrh, or spikenard, acts as a cue to the sub-conscious that we are moving closer to the liminal space between worlds.

Music is perhaps one of most powerful tools for altering consciousness. We experience that nearly daily when we hear a song from the past and are instantly transported to another time. Beyond that, there are musical instruments and recordings designed to ***entrain*** the brain to different levels of consciousness. Entrainment is the tendency for two oscillating bodies to lock into sync so that they begin to vibrate in harmony. It is a universal principle appearing in chemistry, biology, medicine, psychology, sociology and astronomy. It is quite evident in music. [24]

Though the principle of entrainment is attributed to the 17th century Dutch mathematician Christian Huyghens, Tibetan Buddhist monks have used entrainment for centuries. The tingsha is a set of two little brass cymbals of slightly different sizes. When struck together they sound two slightly different pitches, which bring the left and right hemispheres of the brain together and improve meditation.[25]

In the 21st century, there are musicians and recording companies that create music with the principle of **entrainment**, using binaural sound to synchronize brainwave activity and facilitate attaining various levels of consciousness. Some are listed in the Resources List at the end of this book. It is highly recommended that several of these be purchased and used to help train the brain.

---

24 Jonathan Goldman, *Sonic Entrainment*, from a paper first presented at IV International MusicMedicine Symposium, 1989, at Rancho Mirage, California.

25 Ibid.

Each layer of sound, sight, smell, and texture will act as a trigger to your subconscious. Repetition will deepen your experience.

Remember, we–our consciousness, our souls, and our spirits—are our instruments. We are the hollow bamboo through which God plays. We first set the stage; then our spiritual practice tunes our instrument so we can perceive higher and finer levels of consciousness allowing us to access our angel guides and teachers. Next, we will delve deeper into levels of consciousness such as those of coma patients to establish rapport and perhaps even communicate. With that goal in mind, there are some elements essential to this work that should be part of one's spiritual practice if they are not already. We will address those in the next section.

THE PROCESS

The following series of spiritual warm up exercises is called "the process." This warm up is to be done daily, just like professional dancers take a daily class to continue strengthening their technique and honing their abilities. This is a template that can be adjusted to fit each person's individual spiritual belief system, but the steps remain the same. It is suggested that this template be followed for at least a year or two before improvising your own.

We'll look at each of the steps in their proper order.

Prayer - This is the first step in charging our connection to source, to divine consciousness, to the God of our understanding. When we pray, we link up with the "I am that I am." We begin to align ourselves with our highest image of God. Prayer establishes a channel and begins opening it. We open to and invite a conversation with God. Any prayer that is potent and personally meaningful is appropriate. Practice praying aloud, as the powerful vibrations set in motion by your voice will strengthen the vessel you are creating. Below are several prayers from different traditions that you may find inspirational.

The Lord's Prayer
Adapted to energize the chakras by Edgar Cayce

Mother/Father God who art in Heaven (third eye)
Hallowed be thy name (crown)
Thy kingdom come, Thy will (throat) be done,
In Heaven, so on Earth.

Thank you this day for our bodily needs, (root)
And for forgiving us our trespasses, (solar plexus)
As we forgive those who have and do trespass against us.
And for being Thou the Guide (sacral), in times of turmoil, temptation and trouble.

Leading us to paths of Righteousness (heart): right heart, right attitude, right purposes,
For thy namesake. (crown)

A Guide to the Bodhisattva's Way of Life
Shanitdeva

May I be the doctor, the nurse, and the medicine
For all the sick beings in the world
Until everyone is healed.

May a rain of food and drink descend
To clear away the pain of thirst and hunger,
And during the aeon of famine
May I myself change into food and drink.

May I become an inexhaustible treasure
For those who are poor and destitute;
May I turn into all things they could need,
And may these be placed close beside them.

Prayer of Peace

St. Francis of Assisi

Lord, make me an instrument of your peace,
Where there is hatred, let me sow love;
where there is injury, pardon;
where there is doubt, faith;
where there is despair, hope;
where there is darkness, light;
where there is sadness, joy;

O Divine Master, grant that I may not so much seek to
be consoled as to console;
to be understood as to understand;
to be loved as to love.

For it is in giving that we receive;
it is in pardoning that we are pardoned;
and it is in dying that we are born to eternal life.

Angels of the Elements Prayer

Omraam Mikhaël Aïvanhov

Almighty Lord God, Creator of heaven and earth, Master of the universe, send me your servants, the angels of earth, water, air and fire, so that I may work with them for the coming of your kingdom and your justice.

May the Angel of Earth absorb all that is unclean in my physical body, so that I am able to carry out your will and express your splendour!

May the Angel of Water wash my heart of all impurities, so that it becomes a receptacle of your infinite love! May the Angel of Air purify my intellect, so that it shines with your light and your wisdom!

Finally, Lord, send me the Angel of Fire, that it may sanctify my soul and my spirit, so they become the dwelling place of your truth!

She Who Heals

American Indian Prayer

Mother, sing me a song
That will ease my pain,
Mend broken bones,
Bring wholeness again.

Catch my babies
When they are born,
Sing my death song,
Teach me how to mourn.

Show me the Medicine
Of the healing herbs,
The value of spirit,
The way I can serve.

Mother, heal my heart
So that I can see
The gifts of yours
That can live through me

Native American Prayer of Healing

In the house made of dawn.
In the story made of dawn.
On the trail of dawn.
O, Talking God.
His feet, my feet, restore.
His limbs, my limbs, restore.
His body, my body, restore.
His mind, my mind, restore.
His voice, my voice, restore.
His plumes, my plumes, restore.

With beauty before him, with beauty before me.
With beauty behind him, with beauty behind me.

With beauty above him, with beauty above me.
With beauty below him, with beauty below me.
With beauty around him, with beauty around me.

With pollen beautiful in his voice, with pollen beautiful
in my voice.
It is finished in beauty. It is finished in beauty.
In the house of evening light.
From the story made of evening light.
On the trail of evening light.

Prayer for Freedom from Suffering

The Buddha

May all beings everywhere plagued
with sufferings of body and mind
quickly be freed from their illnesses.
May those frightened cease to be afraid,
and may those bound be free.

May the powerless find power,
and may people think of befriending
one another.

May those who find themselves in trackless,
fearful wilderness—
the children, the aged, the unprotected—
be guarded by beneficent celestials,
and may they swiftly attain Buddhahood.

Hindu Prayer for Peace

Oh God, lead us from the unreal to the Real. Oh God, lead us from darkness to light. Oh God, lead us from death to immortality. Shanti, Shanti, Shanti unto all. Oh Lord God almighty, may there be peace in celestial regions. May there be peace on earth. May the waters be appeasing. May herbs be wholesome, and may trees and plants bring peace to all. May all beneficent beings bring peace to us. May thy Vedic Law propagate peace all through the world. May all things be a source of peace to us. And may thy peace itself, bestow peace on all, and may that peace come to me also.

Prayer for Kindness

Bahá'u'lláh

Be generous in prosperity, and thankful in adversity. Be fair in thy judgment, and guarded in thy speech. Be a lamp unto those who walk in darkness, and a home to the stranger. Be eyes to the blind, and a guiding light unto the feet of the erring. Be a breath of life to the body of humankind, a dew to the soil of the human heart, and a fruit upon the tree of humility.

Sufi Prayer for Peace on Earth

Hazrat Inayat Khan

Send Thy peace O Lord, which is
perfect and everlasting,

that our souls may radiate peace.
Send Thy peace O Lord,
That we might, think, act and speak harmoniously.

Send Thy peace O Lord, that we
may be contented and thankful for
Thy bountiful gifts.

Send Thy peace O Lord, that amidst
Our worldly strife, we may enjoy Thy bliss.

Send Thy peace O Lord, that we
may endure all, tolerate all, in the thought of
Thy grace and mercy.

Send Thy peace O Lord, that our lives
May become a Divine vision and in Thy light
All darkness may vanish.

Send Thy peace O Lord, our Father and Mother,
That we Thy children on Earth may all
unite in one family.

Setting an Intention – Intention rightly used is a powerful tool for creating what we want. Science is beginning to confirm what mystics have long known: that creation flows from thought. Our thoughts are the building blocks of our reality. We can create by default or by conscious choice. Setting an intention creates the mold into which the infinite will pour, so it is important to consciously set our intention and set it high. Make it the grandest vision imaginable. This can be for the overall purpose of our life and also for the day. It is important that we also set the vibration for our work as death midwives, so a simple statement addressing how we wish to fulfill this role is very helpful.

Take a moment and ask yourself, "What is my highest soul desire?" You are asking your soul, your highest self, what it would like to manifest in this life. If the answer comes back, "That snazzy red Mercedes sport coupe," it is a good indication that it is not your soul talking. Begin a dialogue with your soul and listen to what it tells you. Your intention will evolve and grow as you do, so allow it the freedom to do so. Again practice stating your intention aloud, knowing that you are shaping the mold for the vessel you are creating.

Surrendering – This can be a difficult step for many, but it is essential. The idea of surrender runs counter to our modern western culture, which tends to mistake it for weakness, lack of drive, or indecisiveness. In fact, it is just the opposite. It takes a truly strong person of faith to surrender to divine will. It takes courage and certainty to trust that if we do surrender to "that which is greater than ourselves," we will be supported and guided and nurtured. As death midwives, we are servants of God and of our sacred charges. In true humility we must surrender to divine consciousness. We sincerely ask that Source use us in this important work. Our will aligned with divine will is our strength, our surety, and our protection. Again, voicing our surrender aloud is important and very powerful. You can experiment with statements of your own choosing or with the following:

"I surrender my life, my soul, and my work into Your hands. Guide me, teach me, use me. Thy will, entwined with my will, be one. I offer my body as a conduit for the descent of divine light and love. I offer my mind as a conduit for the descent of divine light and love. I offer my heart as a conduit for the descent of divine light and love." Try to really feel your soul opening to the divine and, as you do, know you are simultaneously creating the opening of the vessel.

Charging the Connection to our Higher Selves, Angels, Guides, and Master Teachers - It is a mistake to presume that we do any of this work alone. Knowingly or unknowingly, we work with the assistance of our higher self, angels, guides, and master teachers. In truth, this work cannot be done alone. It will serve us well to make this connection consciously, to knowingly seek and rely on the guidance and support of our non-physical helpers. The power of imagination is one of the death midwife's most vital tools. By actively using imagination we charge up and strengthen our connection to our non-physical support group. We must request their assistance with gratitude and love, as they will not impose themselves upon us or upon this work. We must ask, trusting that they will always say yes. Nevertheless, it is our job to become more and more aware of and receptive to their guidance.

How do we develop a relationship with our angelic guides and teachers? The same way we develop a relationship with anyone. We first let them know we are aware of them and that we welcome their friendship, tutelage, and support. Send out an invitation to the guardian angels and guides that agreed to be your special connections to spirit from the beginning of time. Let them know that you are actively seeking their friendship and their communion now.

It is important to set boundaries: We are seeking guidance from the highest entities with which we can be in vibration. We only want contact with those non-physical beings that are in accord with our highest good and with the service we offer. We need to keep focused on the highest, the purest, the finest, and then be discriminating as we develop our relationship with these spiritual helpers. We would not take instruction or advice from just anyone in the physical world, and we should be just as discerning with our relationships in the non-physical world.

Be aware. Is the contact loving? Is it respectful? Is it kind? These are some good indications that we are in contact with the higher vibrating energies. As our relationship grows, we will become familiar with the vibrations of our helpers and how they make contact with us. Begin a dialogue with them, have conversations, share thoughts and feelings, ask them questions and then pay attention to the various ways they may answer. Watch for dreams or seemingly coincidental events – a song on the radio or a line from a movie that seems to speak the answer. A book falls off the shelf. It just might have the answer you seek. Inspiration comes unbidden. For me, it is while soaking in a long hot bath, essential oils wafting on the steam, that a great deal of inspiration from and communication with my angels come. Be open to the many ways they may choose to commune with you.

Most of all, understand that a good relationship with angels and other non-physical teachers and guides is like a good relationship in the physical – it takes commitment and time to develop trust and love. As our relationship with our personal non-physical collaborators strengthen, so does our vessel, so does our conduit.

Creating the Healing Circle – This can be done any day but is critical on days when we actively serve the dying. This service is active on many planes, so even at times when we are not physically able to assist the dying, we can assist them on the inner planes. Therefore, it is vital to create the healing circle on any day we wish to serve, whether or not we are physically present with our patient.

Begin by getting into a contemplative, receptive state and, if possible, speak aloud. Create a healing circle by calling in the higher self of the dying person and of everyone who might play a part in that person's transition. If the person is in a hospital, this might include doctors, nurses, social workers, chaplains, aides, technicians, food servers and janitors. It also includes all family members, specifically those who will play a part in the dying person's care and decision-making. We also call in the guardian angels of all involved. Then we invite the archangels, specifically Michael and Raphael. It is also good to invite any with whom you've created a special bond—or you can just play it safe and invite all of the archangels. Those who are needed will attend. Then call in any master guides and teachers who may be willing to assist in the work. (If you will be serving more than one person that day, include each person's higher self, caretakers, and family.)

Place the patient or patients in the center of the circle. Next, visualize yourself, the higher selves of all involved on this plane, as well as the guardian angels, archangels, guides, and teachers from the non-physical, forming a circle around the patients. We place all patients inside the circle whether or not we are physically able to see them this day. That way the work can continue on the inner planes no matter what. See and feel those in the center of the circle suffused with light and love. See the fire of white light burn away anything that isn't for the highest good of those in the center of the circle. See and feel all those gathered in the center of the circle and those surrounding them joined as one cohesive unit, one heart, one mind, one soul. Then set the intention that we come together to create a sacred space for perfect healing, whatever form that healing may take for each individual.

Once that is done, we ask that we be made clear and pure conduits through which divine energy may flow. We ask that we be able to direct and focus that divine flow with ease to the one making his transition. We acknowledge that we are not the healers but merely the pure conduit through which Source flows.

Next we ask Archangel Michael to cut any energetic cords between us and the person dying when we leave his room, allowing that energy to return to its rightful owner with love. Even though we will do this for ourselves upon exiting each room, we ask for Michael to look out for us, as sometimes, in the intensity of the moment, it is easy to forget.

It is always good, but most especially if we are working in a hospital, to ask Archangels Raphael and Michael to help strengthen our physical, emotional, mental, and spiritual fields, making them strong, resilient, and protected from any undesirable force, be that infection of the body or doubt, fear, or worry. This helps those of us who are empathic to resist taking on all the suffering of our patients.

Finally, we thank all those gathered for joining us in this sacred endeavor and for strengthening our vessel.

Breathwork – The next four steps in "the process" tune our vessel as a musician tunes her instrument. Some form of breath work is highly desirable, be it Eastern pranayama or simple diaphragmatic breathing. There are many books and breath-work facilitators that can help if you have no knowledge or experience with breathwork. Making this a part of daily practice clears out a lot of emotional debris from our energy fields so we come to the work in as pure a state as possible. It also helps to charge and vitalize our fields with life force—pure prana in the yogic system, chi in the Chinese, or rauch in the cabalistic traditions.

While it is beyond the scope of this book to fully explore the many techniques of breathwork, here are a couple of basic techniques, suitable for the work we do as death midwives.

Four Part Breath - In this first technique, our breath is isolated into four distinct parts: inhalation, holding the inhalation, exhalation, holding the exhalation.

Start by just breathing normally. Do nothing but be a witness to your breath. Notice how you are breathing. Are you breathing quickly or slowly? Deeply or shallowly? Are your breaths smooth or jagged? Is the inhalation longer, the exhalation longer, or are they both about equal in length? Resist judging or changing your breath in any way. Just notice and let it be.

Now, slowly begin to shape your breathing so that you inhale for a count of four, hold your breath for a count of four, exhale for a count of four, and hold your breath again for a count of four. Make the tempo comfortable for you. There should be no straining with this exercise. As you grow more comfortable, you'll notice your breath naturally elongating...so that now your tempo slows so instead of inhaling for the count of four, you now inhale for a count of 6, then perhaps 8, 12, 16...and on. Again, do not force the breath. Allow it to elongate in its own time at its own pace. Keep your focus on your breath and only on your breath, letting all other thoughts settle like sand to the bottom of a still lake. Practice this exercise for 5 minutes to start, gradually lengthening your practice to 10 then 15 minutes or more.

Nadi Shodhana (Alternate Nostril Breathing) - This breathing exercise, or pranayama, comes from the yogic tradition. It helps to bring the left and right brain hemispheres into alignment. Throughout the day, we shift from right hemisphere thinking to left hemisphere thinking but often we tend to favor one side over the other. To help correct this bias, practice the following:

With your dominate hand, fold the index and middle fingers down to touch the fleshy thumb pad. The thumb, ring, and little fingers are extended. Bring the ring and little fingers together so that they are touching. (See photo 1) Bring your hand to your nose. Place the thumb lightly against one nostril, near where the bone ends and the fleshy part of the nostril begins. Lightly place your ring finger on the same place of the other nostril. (Photo 2)

Inhale for a count of four. As you exhale, gently close off one nostril with your thumb, exhaling through your other nostril (ring and little finger side) for a count of four. (Photo 3) Inhale for four counts again through that same nostril (ring and little finger side); then on the exhale, gently close off that nostril (ring and little finger side) and exhale for four counts through the thumb side nostril. (Photo 4) Inhale for four counts through the thumb side nostril again and repeat the exercise. Continue alternating between the left and right nostrils noticing which side breathes more freely and which side is more closed off. Continue the exercise until you feel both sides balance out and you can breathe freely and equally from both nostrils. This can take some time so be patient. Again, keep your focus on your breath to the exclusion of all other thoughts. If your mind wanders, bring it gently back to your practice.

Hand Positions for Nadi Shodhana

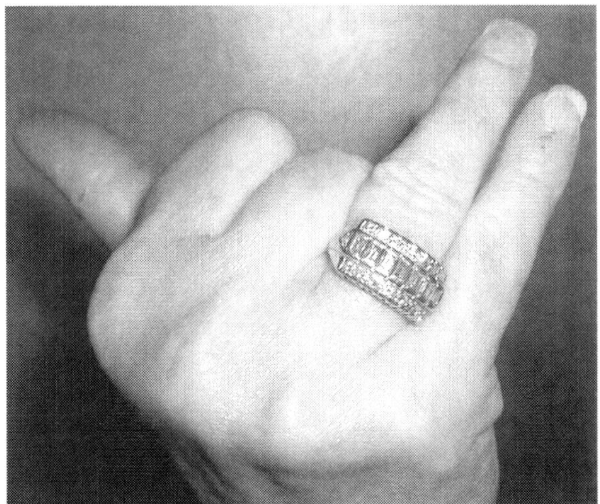

Hand position #1

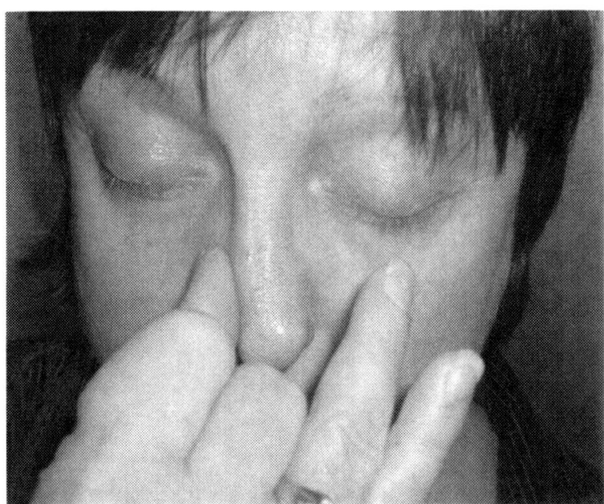

Hand position #2

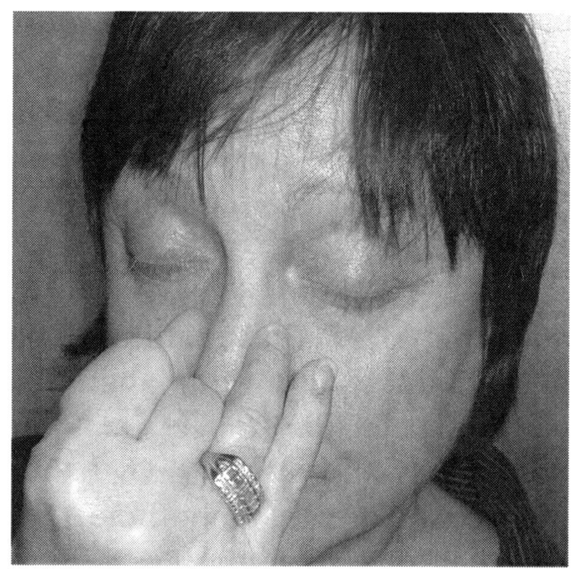

Hand position #3

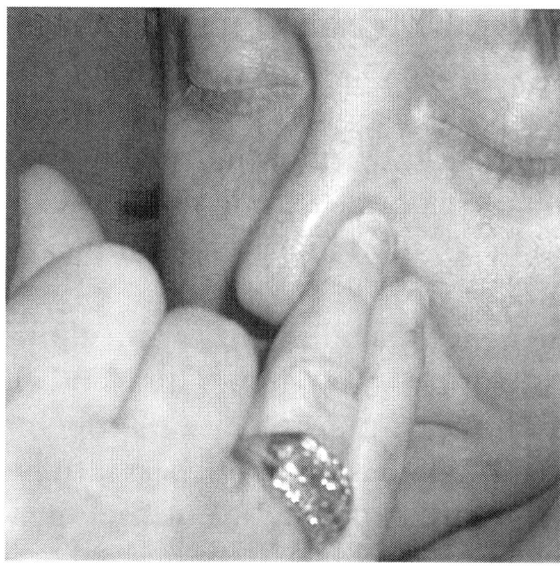

Hand position #4

Chakra Breathing - This next exercise is a bit more advanced so be comfortable with the previous two before going on to this one.

Sit or lie comfortably. Begin by just breathing naturally. Be a witness and do not try to alter your breathing in any way. Again, notice the shape and texture of your breath, just letting it be.

1. Slowly begin to shape the breath…inhaling and filling the belly fully, letting the abdominal muscles relax so your belly fills up like a balloon. Then exhale completely and let the belly balloon deflate. Do not force the breath, but rather invite it into the belly. Do that for several minutes.

2. Now allow the breath to fill your lungs. Invite the breath in, fully expanding your chest and diaphragm. There should be no straining or force whatsoever. Then exhale fully, allowing the chest and belly to deflate and contract, until all air is expelled from your body. Do that for several minutes.

3. On the next inhalation, invite and allow the breath to fill the upper chest, upper lung and clavicle area. Do not force, but just create the opening for oxygen to fill. When the upper chest is fully expanded, exhale gently expelling all of the air. Do this for several minutes. Notice if there is a pause at the top of the inhalation and/or at the bottom of the exhalation. If there is, it may gradually increase with

practice. If there is not, t witness to the unfolding of yo to even out the breath so that th hale are the same length. This is breathing.

4. Now, continuing the full diaphragma ing, inhale fully, and on the exhale, gen your breath on your root chakra at the your spine and visualize yourself exhaling in Feel your breath entering the root chakra, en ening it, recharging it, rebalancing it, cleansing it, and purifying it. Repeat this for several breaths, gently exhaling into the chakra. If you can visualize that with ease you may want to add seeing the chakra charged with the color red. Notice anything that happens while you do this and breathe into any sensations, images, sounds, or emotions that arise.

5. Release your breath and all visualizations. Just let your breath do whatever it wants to for a minute or so. Over time, this will free up your innate breath—that deep, full, unobstructed breath we all enjoyed naturally as infants.

6. Bring yourself back to the full diaphragmatic breathing once more and exhale gently into the sacral chakra, located above the root chakra about two inches below your navel, charging, clearing, and

evitalizing it. When you are comfortable, visualize the color orange. Repeat this for several breaths.

. Release the breath again, allowing your innate breath to unfold for a minute or so.

8. On the next exhalation, exhale into the solar plexus chakra near the bottom of your ribcage. Gently exhale into it, eventually adding the color yellow.

9. Return to your innate breath.

10. Exhale into the heart chakra in the center of your chest, adding the color green when you are able.

11. Return to your innate breath.

12. Exhale into your throat chakra, adding the color blue.

13. Return to your innate breath.

14. Exhale into your third eye chakra located between your eyebrows. Add the color indigo.

15. Return to your innate breath.

16. Exhale into your crown chakra adding the color violet.

17. Return to your innate breath.

18. Finally, inhale fully, drawing the breath from the bottoms of your feet, all the way up, seeing the color of each chakra as you reach it until you send the breath out through the top of your head, at which point you visualize a white fountain of light showering down upon you and circling back to your feet. Take several breaths, drawing the breath, along with this white light, up through all of the chakras feeling them radiating energy and balance.

Meditation – Whatever form of meditation that resonates is appropriate. The goal is to reach a very quiet place in the mind, turning down the volume of the ego, while turning up the volume of the Higher Self.

The simple act of witnessing the breath without trying to control it in any way is one of the simplest and most profound forms of meditation. Created by Guatama Buddha, this meditation is called Vipassana.

The four part breath or the Nadi Shodhana pranayamas can also be used as meditation techniques as can the many moving meditations, such as yoga, tai chi, or qigong. Gazing at a lighted candle can help focus and quiet the mind. Silently repeating a mantra can be helpful. From the Eastern tradition, you can experiment with sacred sounds such as *Om, So Hum* or *Sat Nam.* From the western tradition you can experiment with *Shalom.* No one size fits all when it comes to meditation. What is important is finding the technique or techniques that work best for you. If meditation is something new for you, begin practicing for five minutes and slowly lengthen the practice to about twenty minutes.

Mindfully Raising our Vibration – The first part of the process up to now has helped us to warm up and access the lower, slower states of consciousness but now we will engage to access the higher ones. In the beginning, this may feel a little abstract, but with practice, we learn how mindfully raising our vibration feels. It will be different for each of us. Understand that there are many ways to raise our vibration and any way that works for you and feels good is right. Be open to experimenting with different ways to achieve this. The more ways we can access this raised rate of vibration, the better.

After meditation, state internally the intention to raise your vibration as close as is safely and humanly possible, to match God's. We will never reach that ultimate frequency, but with dedication, devotion, and practice, we can consciously raise our vibration higher and higher. The goal is to tune ourselves up until, like a Stradivarius violin, we are able to reach notes beyond human hearing. These higher levels of vibration, higher levels of brainwave activity and consciousness are where, I believe, we come into contact with our angelic assistants. We will discuss the various levels of consciousness in greater detail later. For now just know that we want to open our range of consciousness as fully and freely as possible.

To raise your vibration, begin a type of breathing where the inhale is deep, full, and unstructured. On the exhale, engage a kind of pressured toning in the back of the throat with the glottis partially closed, similar to the ujjayi breath of yogic pranayama. Imagine you are fogging up a pair of glasses but with the mouth closed. The sound is like the ocean in a conch shell or the hissing of a cobra. Simultaneously, visualize or feel yourself rising up. Continue this specialized breathing while experimenting with the following two visualizations to see which is more effective. In time, you may improvise your own unique methods of accessing this state.

Riding the Silver Cord

With eyes closed, see yourself lying or sitting where you are doing your process work. Imagine a silken, silver cord attached to your body and extending infinitely upwards into the heavens. Hold onto the cord. See and feel yourself rise up this ethereal silver cord, higher and higher into the night sky until the stars and sky fade away and you are in pure white light.

The Heavenly Elevator

Imagine a beautiful elevator before you. There are several stairs than must be climbed to reach it. Inside the elevator, the ornate platinum filigree doors close. Above, the ceiling is transparent, the night sky ablaze with stars.

Your fingers press the lighted buttons for the different "floors." These are different levels of consciousness. Higher and higher you go, watching the night sky and stars disappear until there is only a pure white light.

These are just examples that give an idea of what we might visualize to raise our vibration. What is important is to color these visualizations in great detail and depth, to make them as real as possible. Our brains do not know the difference between what we see with our outer eyes and what we see with our inner eyes. Both are reality for our brains. Imagination is the key to unlocking these inner planes, which are so vital in our work with the dying; so let it create in vivid detail using as many senses and textures as possible.

While mindfully raising your vibration, be very aware of sensations. In time, you will become familiar with signals that tell you that your vibration is rising while at the same time maintaining contact with the slower states of consciousness. I can tell when my consciousness is opening up and reaching both higher and lower states by feeling several things. First there is a sense of counterbalanced movement, the feeling of being stretched upwards while at the same time being equally pulled downwards, almost in a kind of traction or like a salt water taffy pull. This tells me that as I am accessing the higher realms of my angels, guides, and teachers, I am also reaching into the deeper realms of consciousness where those who are transitioning from this world into the next often travel.

Think of sounds waves...the highest and lowest waves we humans cannot hear, while dogs hear some of the highest and whales converse on some of the lowest. We are extending our consciousness into those realms with this practice.

Chanting – Another great way to raise our vibration is through chanting. The sounding of sacred words and vowels creates powerful energies within our bodies. These tune and uplift our physical vehicles to a finer and finer degree. Anyone can chant. Being a great singer isn't required. Being able to vibrate your whole being with sacred sounds is. There are many sacred sounds and words from many various traditions.

The simplest and easiest from the eastern tradition is chanting the word "Om." It is considered to be the primal sound or vibration from which the entire universe constantly emanates. From the western tradition, we have "Shalom" which not only means peace but also bestows the highest blessings for the most beneficent outcome for all concerned. Note how both words have the sound "Om." This one sound is of tremendous positive power. It is worth contemplating upon the unity in diversity that these two sacred words imply.

For charging the chakras, one series of chants from an eastern tradition and one from a western tradition are included here to get you started. As always, experiment and find the words or sounds of power that work best for you.

Eastern Technique – Bija Mantra[26]

This mantra, called a "seed" mantra is chanted to activate the chakras. Begin with the first chakra and end with the sixth chakra. There is no bija mantra for the seventh chakra as, in this instance, it is considered the center of liberation. The idea is to focus your attention upon the sacred sounds, feeling your whole body vibrating with them. Pay special attention to the corresponding chakra. First chant the sound on whatever note feels best to you. Play with it until you find just the right note for each sound. Later you may chant the word on the note listed for each chakra. A pitch pipe, found at most music stores, would be helpful for finding the recommended notes.

Sound	Chakra	Position	Lotus	Name	Note
LAM	1st	root of spine	four-pettaled	Muladhara	C
VAM	2nd	sacral	six-pettaled	Svadhisthana	D
RAM	3rd	solar plexus	ten-pettaled	Manipura	E
YAM	4th	heart	twelve-pettaled	Anahata	F
HAM	5th	throat	sixteen-petalled	Vishudda	G
OM	6th	third eye	two-petalled	Ajna	A

26 Anonymous. (2002) *Meditations on the Tarot; A Journey into Christian Hermeticism.* New York, NY; Jeremy P. Tarcher/Penguin, pg. 227.

Western Technique[27]

Chant from the first chakra to the 7th chakra. Begin by experimenting to find the right note for each phrase. Then experiment with the given note for each phrase.

Phrase	Chakra	Position	Note
I am the vine	1st	root of spine	C
I am the truth, the way and the life	2nd	sacral	D
I am the door	3rd	solar plexus	E
I am the bread of life	4th	heart	F
I am the good shepherd	5th	throat	G
I am the light of the world	6th	third eye	A
I am the resurrection and the life	7th	crown	B

Note – The pressured breath/visualization or chanting technique or both may be used to mindfully raise the vibration. Play with them and find what works best, always being open to changing as the situation requires.

Opening to Receive – Once we raise our vibration as high as we are safely able, we open to receive inspiration and communication in whatever form is appropriate for us. This could be images, sounds, sensations, or information

27 Ibid, pg. 228.

downloaded directly into our consciousness. There are infinite ways the angels, guides, and teachers might use to communicate with us so we must be open—yet always discerning. Communication with our highest self, angels, and master teachers will always be of a loving and helpful nature so we must be wary if any information we receive is not of the highest and purest tone. If we have prepared ourselves thoroughly, this should not be a problem, but it is worth noting as a precaution.

This is also a good time to ask any questions about the service we are to offer. If we need clarity concerning the best way to serve an individual, this is the time to ask for that guidance and know that it will be given if we are open to receiving. Our part in this step is to allow communication to flow freely yet be discerning as to its source.

Inviting – As we begin to return from our time communing with Source and our guides, we invite divine consciousness (the God/Goddess of our understanding, the Christ consciousness, Buddha consciousness, etc.) and our highest self to enter us as fully and as deeply as we are safely able to withstand. With practice, we will be able to house more and more of this God force. Think of being a sacred vessel, a holy grail into which this divine energy flows, filling each chakra from the crown to the root with dazzling white and golden light. Feel it fill you with love and light. Feel it enliven every cell and fiber of your being. Drink deeply from the ever-flowing light and love and become drunk on the divine. Dance with God.

Delight in the remembering that we are one with Source. With practice, this can be an incredibly ecstatic experience. Remember though that we must sincerely offer the invitation, for the divine will never force itself upon us.

Maintaining the Vibration – Once we feel full of divine energy, we set the intention to maintain this higher frequency, using it as a foundation from which to build ever higher with each additional practice.

Charging our Field with the Higher Vibration – We then circulate this energy throughout our body, sending it out into our auric field to repair, renew, strengthen, balance, heal, charge, energize, and sensitize it as well as to release any blockages

Sending the Higher Vibration out into the World – Next, send this benevolent energy outward, sensing a link with the energy of all others who work for the betterment of this world. Dedicate the efforts of this practice to the uplifting of all sentient beings. See this energy flow like a soft blue blanket around the earth, enveloping it with its loving protection and warmth. Send this energy to the leaders of all nations…to those we may think of as friends and those we may think of as enemies in the knowledge that we are, in truth, all one. We are all connected. We are all in this together.

Giving Thanks and Closing – Finally, give thanks and express gratitude to the Mother/Father God of your understanding, to the angels, guides, master teachers, and all who help us on this path. Also give thanks to those who allow us to share in this most sacred time in their lives. Close the process in any way that feels appropriate to you. A simple "Amen" or "Namaste" can suffice.

That is the template for "the process." At first, it may take some time to do each step, but with practice it will flow quite naturally from one step to the next like graceful choreography. Do not rush through it. Be playful with the process while becoming familiar with it. Just as a dancer must strengthen his muscles by practicing each exercise over and over, so must we be willing to dedicate the time to make these spiritual exercises a part of our being. The rewards will be great for those who do.

Before moving on, it is paramount to understand that this work does not flow from us but ***through*** us. We do all of this preparation to make ourselves a hollow bamboo through which God can play. It is easy to fall into the trap of thinking that ***we*** are doing something grand. While it is true that we play an important role in this process, never forget that this work is not about us. Guard against any temptation to think otherwise. All of this preparation is to empty ourselves of our normal state of being, to put ourselves aside, let go of our cares, thoughts, and daily concerns so that we may be a pure, focused, sensitive, and loving presence, receptive enough to allow divine energy to flow through us to the one dying.

Getting the Background

As we prepare our instruments for this work, we must also set the stage. Before we begin our vigil we want to get as much background as possible on the one dying. This would not be necessary if it is a friend or loved one we are companioning; but in a professional setting, it is vital to become as familiar with the patient as possible prior to sitting vigil.

Who is the person you would serve? What is his history? Is he married? Does he have children? How did he make a living? Are there family dynamics that might affect his ability to make this transition? Is there unfinished business? What did he love in life? What is the illness that has brought him to this place? Does he ascribe to any spiritual belief system?

We are like painters who must first have an initial sketch in order to create a full portrait. The more detail we have, the fuller and richer that portrait will be.

If at all possible, get this information directly from the one dying. If that is not possible then understand that any information provided by others—doctors, nurses, social workers, chaplains or family members—comes through their own perceptional filters. Some of this information may have been accurate in the past, but the scene changes constantly as one moves through the spectrum of deathing, so it might not be accurate at the time we enter the sacred space.

This background information can be very helpful in creating a highly individualized and sacred space for the one we serve. It can aid in the creation of metaphors and guided dream walks, can shape the way we phrase or visualize things, and can be put to use if we are inspired to add singing or affirmations. It is very important to get as detailed a history as possible, yet we must be open and flexible enough to trust our own intuition when in the presence of the one dying and adjust accordingly.

DRESSING AS A DEATH MIDWIFE

A few words should be spoken here about choosing the appropriate dress for a death midwife. There are no hard fast rules, but through experience I've found certain things will serve you and your charges well.

First, it is important to have a special set of clothing consecrated to this service and this service only. Think of it as your costume, something that helps get you into your role simply by putting it on. With repeated use, the energy of your service and dedication will intensify in it, marking a clear delineation when entering the liminal space as guide to the souls of the dying.

Think simple lines, simple fabrics, and easy care. Cotton and cotton blends, which breathe, are a good choice. The clothing should be loose fitting and comfortable while sitting, bending, squatting, etc. A good choice might be a pair of slacks, a comfortable top, and perhaps an overcoat that can be removed. Avoid nylon stockings. Sturdy comfortable shoes with good support are really important.

Think about color and patterns. We want to soothe and comfort, not distract and irritate. Solid colors are preferable to busy prints. Look to shades of blues, greens, pinks, and purples rather than reds, oranges, yellows and black. Simple clothing like this can be found nearly anywhere, but uniform stores will have an abundance of nursing scrubs that will suit very well and are reasonably priced.

Once we have performed our morning process work and are in our consecrated clothing, we can travel to the setting where the one we serve resides to begin creating a sacred space.

CREATING SACRED SPACE FOR THE DYING

There is a dignity in dying that doctors should not dare to deny.

– Anonymous

For most people the ideal would be to die at home surrounded by loved ones. It is often the easiest place to create and maintain sacred space. Unfortunately, not everyone will be able to die in the ideal setting—and even with a death at home, there can be challenges.

Creating sacred space in a hospital or nursing home environment routinely presents challenges. Hospitals and some nursing homes are not known for their comfort or serenity. In the hospital, we often attend to people who are in the ICU. The patient may have had a long illness allowing her to come to terms a bit with dying; but just as often, the situation has arisen suddenly with no chance for emotional or spiritual preparation. She may be sharing a room with a stranger. Family dynamics are often complicated, and the medical staff may bring their own unique set of biases. All of these nuances must be taken into consideration and dealt with. As a death midwife, we strive to create a sense of order and peace amidst chaos.

The most important thing we *do* as death midwives is to create and maintain sacred space within frequently challenging environments. We do this to the very best of our abilities, which will be tested and strained in new and different ways each day. We must maintain our balance and the elevated state of consciousness we so assiduously developed in our morning's spiritual process work, while at the same time being able to maneuver the often-stressful atmosphere of a hospital or nursing home and deal with its staff. Frequently we must retune ourselves and become facile at navigating between varying levels of consciousness. This will become easier with practice.

The more we are able to maintain this higher level of consciousness, this connection to Source, the more we will see its effects in the people and situations we encounter. We can create a kind of "Buddha field of energy" that people will feel and respond to, but it takes great discipline. Remember that we invited divine energy, Christ consciousness, and our higher self to abide within us. Let that presence see through our eyes and work through us throughout the day, not just with our patients, but in all of our interactions. Watch how others respond. Even some of the most difficult people can be positively affected by the field of loving intention we create.

ENTERING THE SANCTUARY

Whether in the home, in a hospital, or in a nursing home, whenever possible my preference is to work initially with the patient alone. It is often very difficult to create the space required for this sacred transition when others are present. Once the space is created, however, those in harmony can enter without creating disruption. This is the ideal situation, but we rarely have ideal circumstances in which to work. If the family is in a place of peaceful acceptance, they can sometimes contribute greatly to creating this space. More often, though, the family is raw with grief and there are complicated emotions and dynamics. Honor your intuition in this matter and, if necessary, request or find time alone with the one transitioning.

The one dying can pose challenges to the work as well. Does she know she is dying? Is she able to accept her dying? Does she have issues with anger, regret, fear, or anxiety? All these elements will influence the service we offer. At all times we modify what we offer to fit the need of the one we serve. That is why I find it easiest to work with those who are actively dying. Though they may still have unresolved issues, their conscious defense mechanisms are loosened and their boundaries are more flexible so the focused divine energy we direct has a better chance of being allowed in.

Never forget that people have free will up until the last second of life and can allow or deflect source energy from entering. We engage in a dance of energy as the partner of the one we serve. It is important to understand that the one dying is leading or you might get your toes stepped on. When a person is actively dying, he may be more open to this partnership, but it is not guaranteed. We must respect and honor the patient's right to choose at all times, even when it is hard to do so.

When we enter our charge's room, we need to take time to drink in the present energy. We do not hurry, but stop to sense the energy of the room and those in it. When we feel in alignment, "the practice" begins.

THE PRACTICE

The following steps of the practice should be done in the order given, regardless of the setting.

Introduction - If your charge is conscious, greet her right away and introduce yourself. If the patient is not consciously aware, just be in the space with her for a while before making introductions.

Regardless of their level of consciousness, always, speak to the dying. Understand that whether or not there is a response, the dying can always hear us. Never say anything you wouldn't be comfortable saying to a fully conscious human being.

Ask Permission to Play Music – Always ask permission before playing music. Too often the dying have had their individuality and dignity stripped from them by impersonal institutions and the ravages of illness so we always show respect by seeking permission.

If the person is unable to verbally grant permission, let her know that you will begin playing the music and watch to see if it is all right. Even though she may not be able to respond verbally, she can give subtle clues to indicate whether the music is desired. Tensing of the face or body, increased agitation, etc., may be signs that the music is not welcomed. Watch carefully. With practice, you will become more and more familiar with the many ways those considered unresponsive can communicate. In my experience, the further along on the spectrum of deathing one is, the more open she becomes, and, most often, your offer of music, if properly chosen, will be accepted. Explain that you are going to play some soothing, healing music and that the dying one has only to listen, relax, and allow the music to seep deeply in.

Use intuition to choose the appropriate music and the right volume to begin the session. Check often to see the response to your choice and make changes as needed. In the following chapter we will go into more detail on the importance of music, how to choose it and how to use music and voice in healing.

Clear the Space of Physical Clutter - While the music is playing, we begin shaping the room. First do everything possible to de-clutter the area. Do not touch hospital instruments, but do what can be done to straighten messes, remove or empty overflowing garbage cans, etc.

Close off the Space - Close off the space as much as possible from outside noise. In a hospital or nursing home setting, pull the curtain around the bed for more privacy. Our aim is an open, clear, airy space that is private.

Check and Adjust Lighting – Soft indirect light is preferable. If possible turn off overhead florescent lights. Incandescent is preferable, and if in a home setting, candlelight is optimal. Natural light from the window should be very gentle or diffused. Be sure it is not falling directly on the one transitioning. As much as possible, we want to create a very comfortable safe, quiet, cocoon-like atmosphere. Depending on where the patient is on the deathing spectrum, outdoor scenes from the window might act as an anchor and be unhelpful so use discernment as to whether shades should be open or closed.

Connect with Source – Though in reality we are always connected with Source, it is important to acknowledge and activate that connection at this time. We acknowledge that all divine energy and healing come from the God of our understanding, not from us.

Connect with the Guides – This is the time to reconnect with the guides who will be assisting us. We already established this connection during "the process" so it should be quite easy to revitalize it now. Invite them in. Ask them to guide, assist, inspire, and protect. Notice in what way that connection becomes real and vibrant for you. Do you feel them? Hear them? See them in the astral? Each of us perceives this differently so it's important to know how you make your own special connection to your guides and teachers. With practice your special way of sensing your guides will become clear and vibrant.

Offer Your Body as the Conduit – We ask divine intelligence to use our body as a conduit for the descent of divine light and love. Make that request internally. Repeating it several times helps to deepen the sense of surrendering to divine will in all things. "I offer my body as a conduit for the descent of divine light and love," works very well; but feel free to create this offering in words potent for you. With this statement we acknowledge that light and love flow through us but do not originate with us. We are joining our personal will with divine will. We then focus and direct the flow with our undivided attention and unconditional intention to lovingly serve. That is our purpose and the important part we play in this act of sacred magic.

Charge the Room with Love and Light - **s**tart in one corner and check the energy. Take time to really sense it. It is often very stale and heavy with remnants of distress, pain, fear, and chaos, etc. Begin breathing deeply and fully, then visualize and feel a golden-tinged white light filling the room. Notice how this feels. I feel the light and love flowing quite distinctly from the palms of my hands, from what is known in Qigong as the Lao Gong points, but it can be perceived in many ways.

Pay special attention to the corners where stale energy can collect. Walk slowly around the room and be very thorough. Take time with this practice until you sense the energy lifting, changing, lightening, and enlivening. State aloud or internally as intuition guides the intention to create this sacred space for perfect healing in whatever form that healing may take.

We seek to create a sense of reverence and awe at the possibility of transformation this opportunity presents. We create an energy field that encourages respect, dignity, and support for the one dying. We charge this energy field with the wonder and grace of this birth into a new life. If we do this work conscientiously and with great care, it will become a living presence in the room that others will not fail to feel. In a hospital environment this can be a great challenge, but regardless of the situation, we must diligently endeavor to do it. Everything else we do flows from this field, so with utmost care we must focus all of our attention upon creating and charging this sacred space.

Physically Connect with the Dying – Now it is time to connect with the one we serve. Physical contact, if allowed, is important to help facilitate the flow of divine energy. Beyond that, people are often afraid to touch the dying resulting in touch starvation. That said, touching must be done with care and great respect. Gently ask permission to make light and respectful physical contact. If the patient says no then sit back and make contact on the inner planes. My preference is to make physical contact whenever possible, but with practice we can become strong conduits of the light even without it.

If the patient is unable to verbally give consent, tell her that you will place your fingertips very lightly on her arm and then use your intuitive skills to sense if this is acceptable. Watch very carefully for any signs that it is not acceptable. Do you feel a contraction in her muscles, see a furrowing of the eyebrows, or hear a sound indicating displeasure? If so, release physical contact and make it on the inner planes. With practice, you will be able to read your charge more easily.

Bear in mind that there are times when touch is not appropriate, times when any outer stimulus is too much. When the person dying is moving back and forth between the physical and the non-physical, with shorter and less frequent visits back to the physical, anything that pulls him back to this world—touch, speech, or even some types of music—is counter-intuitive. At all times, we must be very aware and respectful of where the person is on the deathing spectrum.

If permission for touch is granted, it should be very light and on a neutral place such as an arm. Look for a place that will not cause any discomfort. Since the dying deal with enough invasive and unpleasant touch, ours should be respectful, soothing, and reassuring. The lightest touch is required for a good flow of energy. As communion with the one being served deepens, as she begins to trust and open herself more fully, we may be guided to lightly place our fingertips on other parts of the body, most often the top of the head or the heart. That should only happen once the connection deepens and only if we receive guidance to do so.

Body Mechanics

Whether we choose to stand or sit, or a combination of both, is a personal preference. Since we tend to spend long periods of time focusing and directing the flow of light and love, it is usual to sit a good deal of the time. Whichever we choose, it is important to pay attention to body mechanics both for our own health's sake and for a strong and unimpeded energy flow.

When standing, be sure your weight is evenly distributed. Do not sit into one hip or the other. Stay loose. Locked joints will impede the flow of energy. Also make sure that you have an open body position with nothing crossed, shoulders relaxed, neck and head forward to face the patient.

If sitting, be sure that both feet are touching the floor. This helps to keep us grounded. Keep feet, legs, and arms uncrossed. Adjust the chair so that you can face the patient without needing to turn head or twist the torso. Finally, find a way to support your forearms. We'll spend a great deal of time in this position with our fingertips lightly touching the dying so we need support that will not cut off circulation.

You'll feel the need to stretch or change position from time to time. Honor that. Hunch and drop the shoulders several times an hour to release any tension in the neck and shoulders. Move the head right and left, up and down. Contract and release the spine to loosen tension there. Circle the feet and ankles in both directions.

Every movement we do should be in slow motion. We move as slowly and fluidly as we can so as not to disturb the sacred space that continues to deepen. We do not want to inject any disruptive energy into this holy environment with fast and jerky movement so we move as if we are underwater or wading through thick molasses.

Contrary to popular belief, the dying are very sensitive to their environment. As their boundaries become more permeable, they feel our vibrations quite intensely. Many times I've witnessed sacred space desecrated by the harried energy and movements of a frazzled nurse or family member. Often you will actually see the one dying flinch at the entrance into this space by one completely out of tune with the reverent environment we have created. We must do everything we can to make our movements a moving prayer of peace and healing.

Focus and Direct Divine Light and Love to the Dying – Having created a sacred space for perfect healing to unfold, having made connection to our guides and to the dying, it is time to focus and direct divine energy.

Sitting or standing, we close our eyes, go deep within and once again consciously charge our connection to Source, to the God of our understanding with intent, with awareness, and with love. Take the time to feel that connection vibrate with life. It might feel tingly like champagne or buzzing like hummingbird wings. We might see inner lights or hear inner music. It matters not how that connection feels to us as individual sparks of Source; but feeling or sensing this charged connection is important.

As in our previous work, we re-charge our connection to our spiritual family, the angels, archangels, guides, and teachers who have agreed to work with us on this path. Raphael, as the archangel of healing, is especially beneficial. We are never alone on this path of service, and we must never forget that. Take the time to feel your non-physical helpers and gather them close.

Finally we connect energetically with the one dying. We've already made physical contact (if appropriate) and now we establish energetic contact. This will not be too difficult if we come from a place of understanding that, at our fundamental core, we are all one, individuated sparks of God yoked at the most basic level. Feel yourself joining the energetic flow of the one dying. Again take the time to make this connection as real and alive as possible.

Now we want to bring ourselves back to that heightened vibration we achieved during our morning process work. Since we have done the work earlier, it will be easier to access that higher vibration now. Take the time needed to regain that state. With practice, it is like a well-traveled path we can follow easily to the crossroads between worlds.

As we do this, we want to empty ourselves of all of mundane and profane thoughts. We put aside our normal selves and become as hollow bamboo, opening and allowing Source to breathe through us. The less "we" are, the more Source can be. The more room we make inside ourselves, the more Source will fill us. The more we surrender and invite God to work through us, the more God will.

Our biggest job is to be a focused loving presence, a witness to this most sacred intercourse. We concentrate our attention, consciously directing the flow of Source to the one dying. We must not allow our minds to wander. We must be fully present to this miracle, to this mystery. It takes great discipline to stay focused and concentrated for hours at a time, but this is our job. *This* is what we *do.* We stay, we witness, we allow.

Of course, as human beings we are not perfect so we do not berate ourselves if and when we find our focus fading or outside thoughts invade our consciousness. We simply and gently draw our focus and attention back where it belongs. We must remember to treat ourselves with the same love and care we offer to the ones we serve. That is why this is called a practice; we grow stronger and clearer with repetition.

Sometimes when Source energy flows through us, the sensation can be very intense, so powerful as to be startling or possibly even frightening. When that happens, it is essential to remain open and allowing. Remember the morning's process work where we invoked the highest vibration of Source we can safely accommodate and know there is no need to be alarmed. Do not tense against the flow. Just ride the wave, staying loose and trusting that our angel guides and teachers are with us, adjusting our fields as necessary to channel this energy safely. If the energy flow seems too strong to handle, simply ask the angels to slow it down a bit, and they will. Remember always to thank them for their assistance.

Sometimes when Source flows through us it is like a gentle brook, the current barely perceptible. Know that even then, Source is flowing through you to the one in need in just the right amount.

There are many energy-generating healing modalities, but from my own experience, this technique, which draws its source exclusively from the divine without adding any personal energy, is the safest, purest, and most powerful, both for the patient and for us. We should be able to direct Source energy for long periods of time without feeling drained. At first we will need to build up our muscles, in this case, our spiritual muscles, to be certain that divine energy is the only source from which we draw. Initially, we might only be able to stay focused for an hour or so before we feel fatigued. As we grow stronger in our ability, we can remain attentive for longer periods of time. Feeling drained is usually a sign that we've poured our own energy into the mix. This is where practice and discipline come in. By keeping ego out of it and continuing to affirm "Thy will, not mine, be done," we will learn not dilute the flow. True humility will be our best teacher in this.

Dialogue with the Dying - Once we have cleared and charged the energy, created sacred space, connected with Source, our non-physical helpers, and with the one dying, and become a conduit for divine energy, we then open a dialogue. If we listen deeply, the dying will be our teachers. They will tell us what they need. This is rarely done verbally. More often this communication will be at a much more subtle level. It takes skill, sensitivity, and intuition to tune into this communication. Making this contact takes openness and a willingness to delve beneath surface appearances. It takes being able to put oneself aside and quiet the ego enough so that the inner voice of the one dying can be heard. Though this is a dialogue, the most important thing we do is to listen.

This dialogue, if it happens, takes a good deal of time to evolve. It requires we earn the trust of the dying. It is a partnership, as in a *pas de deux*. Like the ballerina who trusts her partner, the dying must trust that we will not drop them. It is a holy relationship. The depth of this relationship will vary with each one we serve. Some souls will connect with us more readily than others. Some will be open to the dialogue and others will not. It is impossible to force another soul into this dialogue. Free will must be honored. Forcing anything, even if we feel it is for the good of the one dying, is an act of violence whose karma we alone will bear.

If a dialogue is established, with skill and practice we can learn to swim in the dying one's stream of consciousness. We do this by internally asking her to draw our spirit to hers. We are already in that more expanded level of consciousness we achieved in our morning process. Now we ask our charge to take us to her current level of consciousness. If our charge is able to talk, she is most likely in a beta or alpha state, and this kind of internal dialogue may not be required. If our charge is unable to respond verbally, we need to move into a deep alpha, theta, or possibly even delta state, and this dialogue becomes our main mode of communication.

It doesn't really matter if we know technically which level of consciousness we are traveling in so long as we have linked with the one we serve. With practice, however, we will become more familiar with how each basic level of consciousness feels.

It takes time to make the link, if it happens at all, and we must be patient and allow it to unfold at its own tempo. Be aware of anything that is noticed, for the conversation may come as images, feelings, emotions, or even scents.

It may also come as an impulse, perhaps an urge to say something to the one dying.

If we are open and aligned, there are many ways the dying can communicate. It takes discernment to know whether the information originates from within us, from the person dying, or from our guides and teachers. If we find ourselves suddenly awash in feelings of anger, frustration, or sadness, there is a good chance that these are waves of emotions emanating from the one dying. When that happens, acknowledge the feelings and let them flow through you. Do not hold onto them or internalize them. We can also offer them to Gaia, to Mother Earth, asking her to recycle and restore them to their highest expression. She is always willing to do this for us if respectfully requested.

We must continually guard against the feeling that we must *do* something. We need to regard that impulse with suspicion. Often it is the voice of ego needing action to feel substantiated. The most important thing we "do" is to *be* in the moment with the one dying, without judgment or agenda. When the patient appears nonresponsive, our role is to be a silent, focused witness to this magical transformation. Just keeping sacred space open so the dying have the room and the support to do what they need to do is a precious gift. Being there for them so they do not suffer from the illusion they are alone is often all that is required. The art of death midwifery is an art of *being* not of *doing*. But just **being** is not easy to **do**.

While it may make us feel more useful, doing just to do is not productive and could even be harmful. **Do no harm** must be our credo, just as it is the physician's. The goal is to create a delicate balance between trusting our intuition and acting with confidence when action is called for. We continually walk the razor's edge, guarding against doing just to do. This balancing act will become easier with practice.

If we have done our preparatory work, we will know a bit about the person we are companioning. This information is the palate with which we begin to paint our conversation. Again, very often this conversation is telepathic rather than verbal. It is important to understand that as someone dies, normal boundaries soften and dissolve, so telepathic communication is not as difficult or unusual as it might seem to our more rational, left brain way of thinking. Be open to the possibility, and witness what happens.

We should at all times be respectful of the belief system of the one dying. If at all possible, we want to know what, if any, spiritual beliefs the person holds and work to the best of our ability within that framework. At the same time, if asked either verbally or telepathically, we may gently and respectfully offer the dying a broader perspective.

For instance, my mother's death transition was severely complicated by the religious beliefs taught to her by her father, a depression era Free Methodist minister. She felt certain she was going to Hell. Needless to say, with that frightening prospect looming, she was not eager to make her transition. Her physical, emotional, mental, and spiritual suffering was excruciating, a living thing with teeth and bloody claws. My brothers and I did our best to assure her, to convince her that God would not judge her so harshly, but she found no comfort in her children's words. We had to find a minister, one close to her faith of origin, to come and speak with her about God's love in a language that resonated with her. Even though he wasn't her father, he symbolized him and did much to help my mother relax and allow the process to unfold with more ease. We must seek to speak the language of the heart for each person or be willing to find those who can.

Our voice is one of the most valuable instruments we have in this work. It is another form of touch, so we want our voices to be a soothing balm that eases fear, anxiety, doubts, or discomfort. It should be like velvet and silk. We can weave a hypnotic lullaby with our words. Quality, pitch, and volume are extremely significant. Our touch and our voice are the predominant avenues by which we connect with the dying in their active stages of transition.

As a trained singer with over 30 years of experience, I have come to know my instrument very well. If you are not familiar with how your voice sounds to others, you must become so. It is wise to record your voice, listen for any sharp edges or nasal intonations, and correct them.

Practice until your voice sounds mellifluous and round like warm honey. A soft volume and gentle tone is needed. The hospital is filled with loud abrasive noises and people prodding the dying with shrill questions as if they were deaf. Never should we add to that cacophony. I cannot tell you how many times I've seen a dying person considered to be "unresponsive" flinch at the sharp tone of a harried nurse. The dying respond not only to the volume, but also to the intention and emotion behind the words. That same nurse may say, "How are you feeling today, Mrs. Smith?" but if the emotion behind her words is really, "I am tired and really don't want to be here," the dying will feel and react to that energy and discount the words. False niceties will not fool the dying, so not only should our voice be gentle and soft, the thoughts and emotions behind the words need to be filled with love and sincerity. Otherwise, instead of comforting, we will offend.

Hearing is the last physical sense to be extinguished. It often intensifies before it burns out. A whisper may be all that is needed to soothe.

There are certain things that the dying may need to hear. Just as the midwife at birth reminds the young mother to breathe, no matter what the outer appearance might be, we remind the one dying that he is secure, that it is safe to let go and that, when the time is right, he can do so easily. This is important because often those closest to the person who is dying are unable to offer that assurance.

The dying are more empowered in the timing of their death than we may realize. It happens often that the one transitioning will wait for the arrival of someone dear or hang on to celebrate an important event. It is not uncommon for the transition to happen in the wee hours of the morning when the patient is alone or when her loved one goes out for a short break. If this is the case, help those left behind to understand that there is no need for guilt.

We die when we are supposed to, and we tend to die in the same manner in which we lived. Unless the opportunity for transformation is embraced, someone who struggled and fought through life is likely to struggle and fight through death. One who faced life's challenges with grace will likely be a graceful partner with death.

As death midwives, we can remind, we can assure, we can assist, we can guide, we can bear witness, but we cannot direct or control this sacred process. That is between those dying and the God of their understanding. Sometimes, as a precious gift, we might catch a brief glimpse into that blessed reunion, and in so doing, we might get a small sense of what our own reunion with the infinite will be.

Gently remind the dying that she is surrounded by a field of unconditional love, the likes of which she may never have experienced on earth. Within that field of love she is never alone. In truth, no one ever really dies alone even when the outer appearances suggest otherwise. There are always angels and other non-physical beings assisting this transformation, but the one dying might not be aware of that. It is our job to remind her.

We also remind the dying that no matter what he might be seeing, or hearing, or feeling, or experiencing, there is no cause to fear. All is well. As one navigates between the two worlds prior to completely crossing over, he might encounter sights, sounds, sensations, and experiences for which he has no frame of reference. Those unusual experiences might cause fear. Our job as death midwives is to assure the dying that this is a normal part of the journey and no cause for alarm.

Use first person statements whenever they are accepted. Be the dying one's voice. Start with something like, "Let my words act as your own…I am safe. I am surrounded by love. I am never alone. There is nothing for me to fear." These "I am" statements are more powerful and immediate than "you" statements. There are some, however, who are so steeped in fear that they will reject "I am" statements. With practice, we will be attuned to this and will switch to "you" statements and see if, in time, the one dying will accept the more direct "I am" statements. Try these both verbally and non-verbally to see which is more acceptable to the one being served.

There are times when we might employ the use of **Dreamwalking.** This technique involves guided relaxation and visualizations to assist the dying in crossing over. They may also be used with those in the earlier stages of dying to establish a safe place to "go" when needing a respite from physical, mental, emotional, or spiritual pain. Dreamwalking will be discussed in more depth in a following chapter.

There may be times when certain rituals are indicated. These are specifically created to suit the needs of the individual and are done only with the permission of the one dying. An excellent book on creating unique rituals for the dying is Megory Anderson's Sacred Dying: Creating Rituals for Embracing the End of Life.

Finally, there are times when any voice at all, no matter how soft or soothing, is too much. This time often comes very close to the moment of the soul's departure from the flesh. At this time, all sound, all music, all voice is an intrusion and a distraction, an anchor to a shore no longer needed. This is the time when silence becomes a symphony of welcome…singing the soul home.

Cutting the Cords - In the ideal situation we, as death midwives, would be with the one dying at the very moment the soul leaves the body and for some time thereafter. Unfortunately, we do not always have ideal situations, and we often find that we must leave a patient before she has fully made her transition. This can be emotionally difficult. Death midwives make very intimate attachments to those we serve, and leaving them while they are still making their transition can, quite understandably, be very stressful. Realistically, we must come to terms with what we can and cannot do. While we may have the opportunity to spend more time in a home setting, it is rare that we are able to finish our work with a patient in a hospital or nursing home setting. It is a simple fact that we must become comfortable with in order to do what we *can* do.

First, remember that despite outer appearances to the contrary, the person dying is never left alone. There are always those angels, guides, and even deceased loved ones that attend them throughout their journey. If we have done our work well, they will have heard us affirm that verbally, telepathically, or symbolically, allowing that message to sink deeply into their subconscious. The dying are in good hands.

Never take on the erroneous burden of thinking you have abandoned your charge. We have only placed them more firmly into the hands of the angels, and there is no better place they can be. We can make that a beautiful part of our taking leave. Start by stating internally that you must leave for now but that you are placing your charge softly and gently into the hands of the angels. This is the gentlest way to begin detaching. Always begin telepathically or symbolically (whichever is most appropriate to the individual situation) before, if appropriate, speaking aloud. Do not doubt for a minute that the dying hear or sense our telepathic communication. The following is an example of just how sensitive the dying can be.

I had a young woman in her early 20s who was dying of cancer. Her relationship with her mother was complicated and distant. I was old enough to be this young woman's mother, and with her obvious (non-verbal) approval and invitation, we quickly bonded. There came a point where she was anxiously thrashing around in the bed filled with anguish and fear. I felt her need to be cradled, to be soothed like a baby, to be fed from an inexhaustible source of love and acceptance. She needed unconditional love and assurance that she was cherished, and it was easy to be a conduit focusing that divine mother love to her. As it flowed, she settled down into a deep, peaceful state, drinking in the love like a thirsty sponge. The time with her flew by in true and sacred communion. When the time came for me to leave, it was tearing my heart out, and yet it had to be done.

Beginning in the gentlest way possible, I sent from my mind to hers the thought that I would soon have to leave, but she was surrounded and supported by a host of angels who loved and would protect her. This was the first step to cutting the cord. Even this most gentle way of detaching was difficult for her…and consequently for me. She heard my thoughts and began to moan, becoming agitated once more. She did not want this communion to end and was letting me know in no uncertain terms. I then began assuring her, verbally, that she was safe, she was surrounded by love, and that she was never alone; then I repeated the soothing mantra until she settled down. This was the second step in cutting the cord.

When we begin our work, we consciously create energetic links to Source, to our angelic team of helpers, and to the patient. When we leave we must gently and lovingly sever the link to our patient. We ask that this cord of energy be returned to the one we serve *at its highest expression,* which is always love. As death midwives in a hospital or nursing home setting, we often see several patients in one day. We must clear the energetic connections from one patient before entering the room of another, not only for the good of the next patient, but also for ourselves.

As empathetic beings, we might have a tendency to absorb the emotions of those we serve. This is not healthy.

It will drain our energy and leave us open to all manner of physical, mental, emotional, and spiritual imbalance. Ultimately we would burn out, becoming useless. If we are to be successful and have longevity in this path of service, we must set firm boundaries.

Be very clear on this point: It is not our energy we give to the patient; it is Source energy flowing through us. Remember that we consciously created this link in order to focus and direct Source energy. Should we make the mistake of channeling our own energy to the one dying, we will not really help that person and, in all likelihood, we will drain ourselves.

It is understood that those of us practicing the art of death midwifery are healthy beings who have worked to increase our vibratory frequency. It is only natural that one who is dying, whose energy is lessening, might try to hook into us in an attempt to draw energy from us. This is not done consciously or with ill intent. It is simply an energetic principle that energy flows from the greater to the lesser.

As part of cutting the cord to the patient, let him know (verbally, if possible) that he is surrounded with love. Verbal reassurance at this time will strengthen the surrounding field of love. Thank him for allowing you to serve. Let him know that it was an honor to be in his presence at this most sacred of times. Put things away, moving smoothly in slow motion, and as quietly as possible, leave the room.

Exiting the Sanctuary - Upon leaving the sanctuary, consciously sever any remaining cords to the patient. Several strong exhales with the intention of sweeping away the energetic ties are helpful, as are hand motions that indicate cutting the cord. Consciously do something physical to break the connection, sending these cords gently back to the patient with love while asking that these energies be restored to their highest vibration. Wash your hands carefully and fully, not only for health reasons, but because this also symbolizes the end of your time together. Be sure to take the time necessary to decompress, rebalance, realign and process the experience before seeing the next patient.

THE DEATHING SPECTRUM

Death is not a noun and not a single moment. It is a verb, and the term deathing would be much more accurate. Rather than a line drawn in the sand that, when crossed, signifies the completion of a life, death is a spectrum that can last for days, weeks, months, or even years. There are cultures where birth is regarded as the beginning of death (see #1 in the following diagram on page 124). In our modern western culture, we tend to think of death as the moment when our respiration, heartbeat, and brainwaves cease to function. That is the arbitrary line in the sand. However, for our purposes as death midwives, we need to understand that death is a process with many stages both before that line...and after.

Regarding birth as our first step towards death, we go about living our daily lives (#2) until something happens, perhaps a terminal diagnosis or life-altering condition (#3). The scenery changes for the dying depending on where they are on the spectrum. In the earlier stages, they may be fully conscious, fully able to respond in the normally defined ways. This is a good time to ask them about their stories, and encourage them to address any unfinished business, do the things they'd like to do, see the things they'd like to see, and spend time with people they love. It is a good time to honor their memories, to encourage them to share what has been meaningful about their life journey, to express their fears or regrets and ask any questions they might have.

As they move forward on the spectrum and their condition deteriorates, the scene changes (#4). The deathing spectrum, however, does not always proceed with a forward motion. Sometimes the one dying will be conscious and clear, focused and alert to the here and now, at other times they are not (#5). Sometimes they may flash back to their past. At other times they may travel to the other shore, taking small "day trips," checking out people and things in the non-physical realm and returning with stories of encounters with people who are dead (#6). To dismiss these stories as hallucinations would not only be disrespectful, arrogant, and distressing to the one dying, it would often be incorrect. The veil between worlds becomes very thin as we move further along the deathing spectrum. For a time, those who are dying straddle two different shores. We should honor the stories they share and feel blessed by the gift of a peek into the realms beyond.

Some times they will appear "unresponsive," (#7). A skilled death midwife may still be able to track and communicate with one at this stage but it is important not to disturb or intrude.

The further along on the spectrum the dying are, the less helpful are things that anchor them to earthly life. Things such as favorite foods, music, scenery, and movies that used to bring comfort may bring sadness or disinterest. The gentle stroking of an arm that once soothed may become annoying. These are signs that the dying one is beginning to detach from this world and start traveling to the other shore.

Continuing to force these once comforting things upon them anchors them to this shore and hinders their progress. You might need to let family and friends know that, although it may be done with love, it is a great hindrance and causes the dying great strife and even suffering. Forcing food or water prolongs physical pain. Statements like, "You can't leave us. You have to fight. I won't be able to make it without you," can create unbearable psychological stress and complicate their death.

A day or so before death, it is not uncommon for the vitals forces of the individual to briefly reassert. An unresponsive person may regain consciousness or a confused person may suddenly become lucid, seeming to be his old self again. This often leads the loved ones to misunderstand the situation and think that perhaps the person will recover. When in truth, what is being witnessed is a beautiful burst of spiritual essence, the moment of conception preceding the birth into a new life, which should be treasured but not misinterpreted as recovery (#8).

Near the moment where the dying cross our imaginary line in the sand, all sound, touch, scent, and sensation may be too intense, too weighty. At that time we should back off, maintaining our vigil silently and without touch. Yet we often continue the mistake of thinking that the dying are unresponsive. That is not true! If anything, they become highly responsive ***to the other shore, to the other realm.*** Like a candle that burns brighter before going out, their senses become heightened before extinguishing altogether. This can turn what was once a soothing experience into an excruciating one for them. We must be certain not to stimulate them at this time, giving them the space needed to make the miraculous transformation from this life into a new life with more ease. Great love requires great sensitivity and sacrifice. Sometimes the greatest gift we can give the dying is the gift of selflessly and gently letting them go.

In our modern culture, once we cross the line in the sand we call physical death - when heartbeat, brainwaves, respiration and all other bodily functions cease, many believe the process ends (#9). However it might serve the dying more fully to consider the likelihood that it does not. There are those who believe the journey continues…either to rebirth, as in the theory of reincarnation, or to higher planes of existence, as in the concept of heaven. How we continue to treat the body and soul of the one crossing to the other shore is just as important as how we treat the dying on this shore.

It is important to maintain a sense of reverence and respect in the moments immediately following the cessation of all bodily functions. I have watched, heartbroken, as families broke out into fights with the body still in the room. Such terrible disrespect to their loved one is due to ignorance! The room where the body lies is still a sanctuary, and everyone in it should behave accordingly. Loud talking and any conversation that is not focused upon the one still transitioning should be conducted outside of this sacred space. We must maintain respect and guard the dignity of the dying at this crucial time and encourage anyone who can't to leave the room.

Also encourage the family to take time with the body rather than rushing to have it taken away. (Some traditions recommend leaving the body untouched for three days.) Of course this is easier at home but most hospitals and nursing homes will honor the family's request to spend some quiet time with the deceased. Consider playing soft transcendent music. Speak to the newly deceased as "Soul of ______," to remind her that she is now disembodied. Keep sending her into the light with prayers and love. Always love.

After the initial three days, once the gradual detachment from the physical body is complete, the soul's journey continues. In the Tibetan tradition, it is believed that the soul goes through a series of states called Bardo experiences in preparation for rebirth (#10). In some Christian traditions, the soul is thought to go to purgatory to become purified for its ultimate reunion with God in heaven. The concepts of purification and reunion with the Infinite are present in some form in most spiritual traditions (#11).

Following the theory of reincarnation, after reunion with the Infinite, the soul prepares for rebirth (#12). There is once again conception - that burst of spiritual essence preceding the birth into physical life (#13). In order to be born into the physical, we must "die" to the non-physical (#1), making birth and death essentially the same—a transition from physical to non-physical and back again. For those who do not accept the theory of reincarnation, the idea of rebirth can be seen in the light of being born into higher and higher levels of heaven. In either case, as we come to understand this process, the fear of death decreases and the awe of transformation expands.

As shown in the following diagram, the deathing spectrum is not linear but circular, with no beginning and no end. In truth, it is a spiral with each successive round evolving higher and higher indefinitely. Consciousness continues—we continue—in different forms, at different levels of existence, eternally and infinitely.

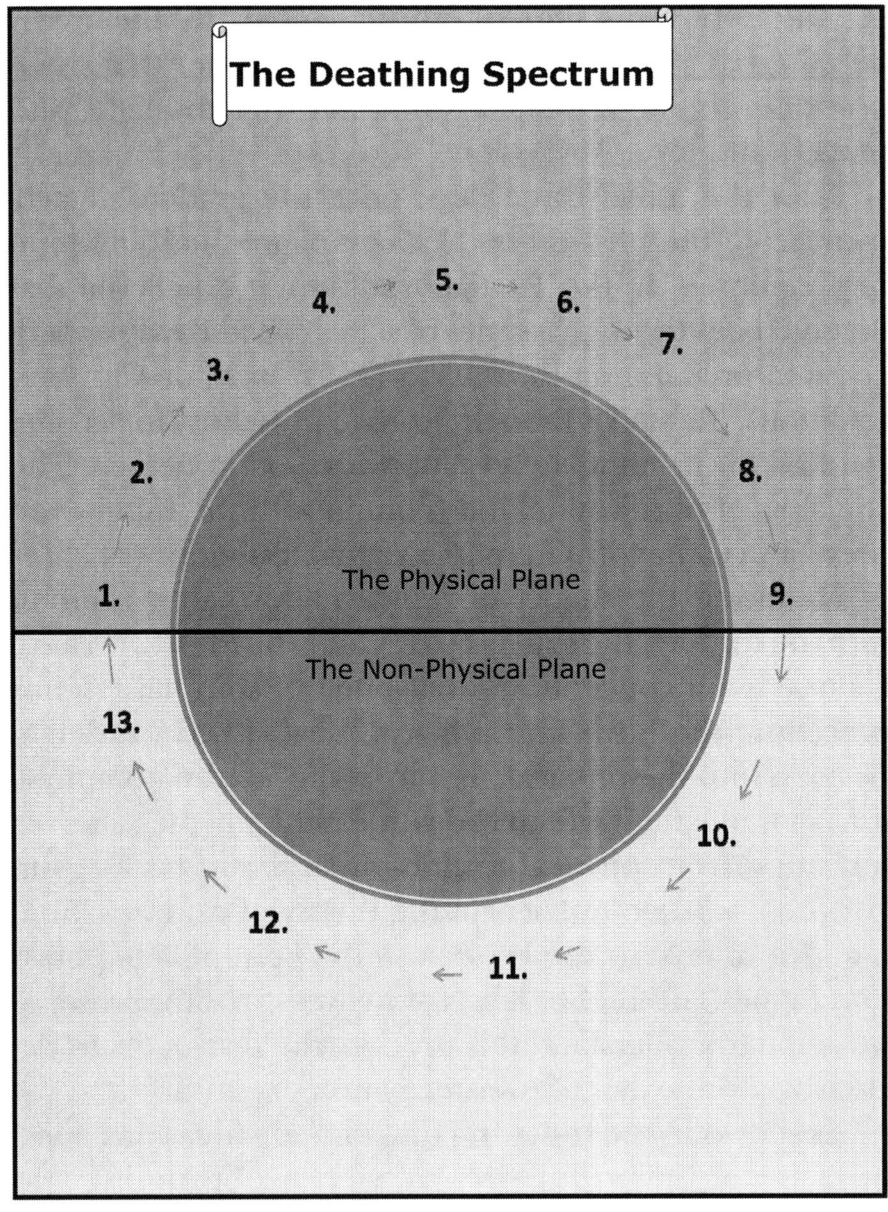
The Deathing Spectrum
1.
2.
3.
4.
5.
6.
7.
8.
9.
The Physical Plane
The Non-Physical Plane
10.
11.
12.
13.

Steps in the Deathing Spectrum

1. Birth into the physical plane/death to the non-physical plane.
2. Life as we normally live it.
3. A life altering event or terminal diagnosis.
4. Our condition deteriorates.
5. We travel through various levels of consciousness.
6. Visits to the non-physical realm
7. Unresponsiveness (We travel back and forth between steps 5, 6 and 7).
8. Burst of life before final withdrawal (conception).
9. Death to the physical plane/birth to the non-physical.
10. Bardo experiences or purgatory.
11. Reunion with the Infinite.
12. Preparation of the Soul for rebirth into the physical.
13. Conception (burst of life).

Beyond Verbal Communication – from the Dying to the Divine

Earlier in the spectrum of dying we may have the benefit of verbal communication with the one we serve; but often that deteriorates with time. Toward the end, the one dying is frequently in an "unresponsive" or coma-like state.

Communication continues to take place, but at different levels of consciousness and in different ways. Part of our work is to be comfortable traveling the terrain of these varying levels, understanding and speaking the language that is fluent there. Our daily spiritual practice should acquaint us with these levels of consciousness and familiarize us with its language.

When working with the dying, we are primarily working with the **alpha** (8-13HZ or 8-13 cycles per minute, see diagram on page 132) and **theta** (4-8HZ or 4-8 cycles per minute) levels of consciousness. Sometimes we traverse the borders of **delta** (.5-4HZ or .5-4 cycles per minute), but that is a deep, dark continent. It takes a lot of practice to remain conscious at the delta level, but it is possible. We'll briefly take a look at each level of consciousness to begin to get familiar with its landscape and signposts.

Beta (13HZ-40HZ or 13-40 cycles per minute) is the state we are most familiar with. It is the state of waking consciousness and active concentration. As the patient progresses on the deathing spectrum, he spends increasingly less time at this level. If we want to get good background information directly from the one being served, we need to connect with our patients while they can still solidly access Beta.

Death midwifery is an art. Artists live and work in the alpha and theta states of consciousness. Not only are these states more conducive to creativity, but from them the illusory boundaries between us become very translucent. The alpha state is one of waking relaxation and daydreaming. The brain waves are slowing down. Meditation often induces an alpha state. Patients in the earlier phases of the deathing spectrum will often reside in alpha, preferring it, even though they can still access beta state and, from time to time, do. While they may choose to respond to us verbally, more often than not, they will choose to communicate in non-verbal ways.

As the brainwaves slow even more, we enter the theta state. It is an even deeper state of relaxation than alpha. Hypnosis brings us to theta. It's the state we access when driving long stretches of monotonous highway, arriving at our destination with no remembrance of exactly what we did to get there. Intuition flows freely in this state that is associated with Shamanic journeying. Therefore theta is the state that opens the door to communicating with those we serve who are no longer verbal.

When the death midwife accesses the theta state, it is possible for him to swim in the stream of the dying person's consciousness. We link up by assessing, as accurately as possible, the level of consciousness at which the dying currently resides; then we match our level of consciousness with theirs. Again, our daily practice should provide us the tools and sensitivity to reach these states much more easily and at will. Keep in mind this is an art, not a science. It is only with practice and dedication that the skill of discerning and matching streams of consciousness will develop.

When the link is made, a kind of mind meld or soul meld begins. Consciously, we link with the one dying, blending, and opening ourselves to a true communion of souls, becoming, for a time, one. Internally ask the one being served, "Bring me to where you are," repeating the request several times until the link is fully established. Depending on the level of consciousness, we might be able to have a "telepathic" dialogue with the dying. We might experience waves of emotions that are not ours. Listen carefully and without judgment. We might receive "promptings," such as "Touch my heart lightly," or "Place your hand lightly on the top of my head," or "Tell me my daughter loves me." If such promptings come from the highest place, if they are of the light and filled with love, then with great respect and caring, follow them.

Sometimes, when working with those in deep coma states, we may find ourselves at the border of the delta level of consciousness. This is the level of our dreamless sleep. It is very difficult to maintain a degree of conscious awareness while in delta, but that is our goal—to walk the edge of the region of deep sleep yet not succumb to it totally. At this level of awareness communication comes in symbols. It takes great finesse to interpret the messages we may receive in this state, and we may never know for sure if we have interpreted them correctly. Practice, sensitivity, discernment, and a willingness to trust our intuition are the keys to successfully traveling the land of delta. It may be useful to keep a journal of symbols received from people in the delta state to see if there are patterns that make sense to you. Your journal may be a first step in learning the symbology of that dark continent.

We discussed the four states of consciousness that the dying will most likely vacillate among. Now we must also consider the levels of consciousness where communication with our angelic guides and assistants transpire. Our task as spiritual death midwives is to develop the skills necessary to travel this full circle of consciousness to the best of our ability.

Current studies of brainwave activity suggest that beyond the four normal states of consciousness at which humans generally function there are both lower and higher levels of activity. These are named epsilon, gamma, hypergamma and lambda.[28]

Below delta state we find **epsilon** (less than .5 HZ) with brainwave activity at one-quarter cycle per second, one cycle per ten seconds, one cycle per minute, and even slower. It is in this extraordinary level of consciousness that one experiences ecstatic states, high degrees of spiritual insight, and even out-of-body experiences.[29]

At the higher end of brainwave activity above beta state resides **gamma** (above 40HZ or 40 cycles per minute),

---

28 Dr. Jeffrey D. Thompson, D.C., B.F.A. (1999), *Epsilon, Gamma, HyperGamma, Lambda and Ecstatic States of Consciousness,* Center for Neuroacoustic Research.

29 Ibid.

hypergamma (nearing 100 HZ or 100 cycles per minute) and **lambda** (200 HZ or 200 cycles per minute). At these more extraordinary levels of consciousness, the right and left hemispheres of the brain apparently synchronize, creating moments of extreme spiritual insight and mystical experience.[30]

Interestingly enough, those in the epsilon state and the hypergamma and lambda states seem to experience the same kinds of spiritual phenomenon. There seems to be a circular link between the very lowest of brainwave patterns and the very highest. Researchers surmise that these divergent patterns form a kind of harmonic blending, creating a continuous circle of consciousness.[31] (see diagram)

Perhaps this is the angelic chorale invoking the music of the spheres. Perhaps as we train our brains to reach ever higher and lower frequencies, we will cross the dimensional boundaries that at this time may seem impenetrable. It is also worth meditating upon the idea that both the deathing spectrum and the frequency spectrum form circles, or more accurately, spirals, with no discernable beginning or end.

30 Ibid.

31 Ibid.

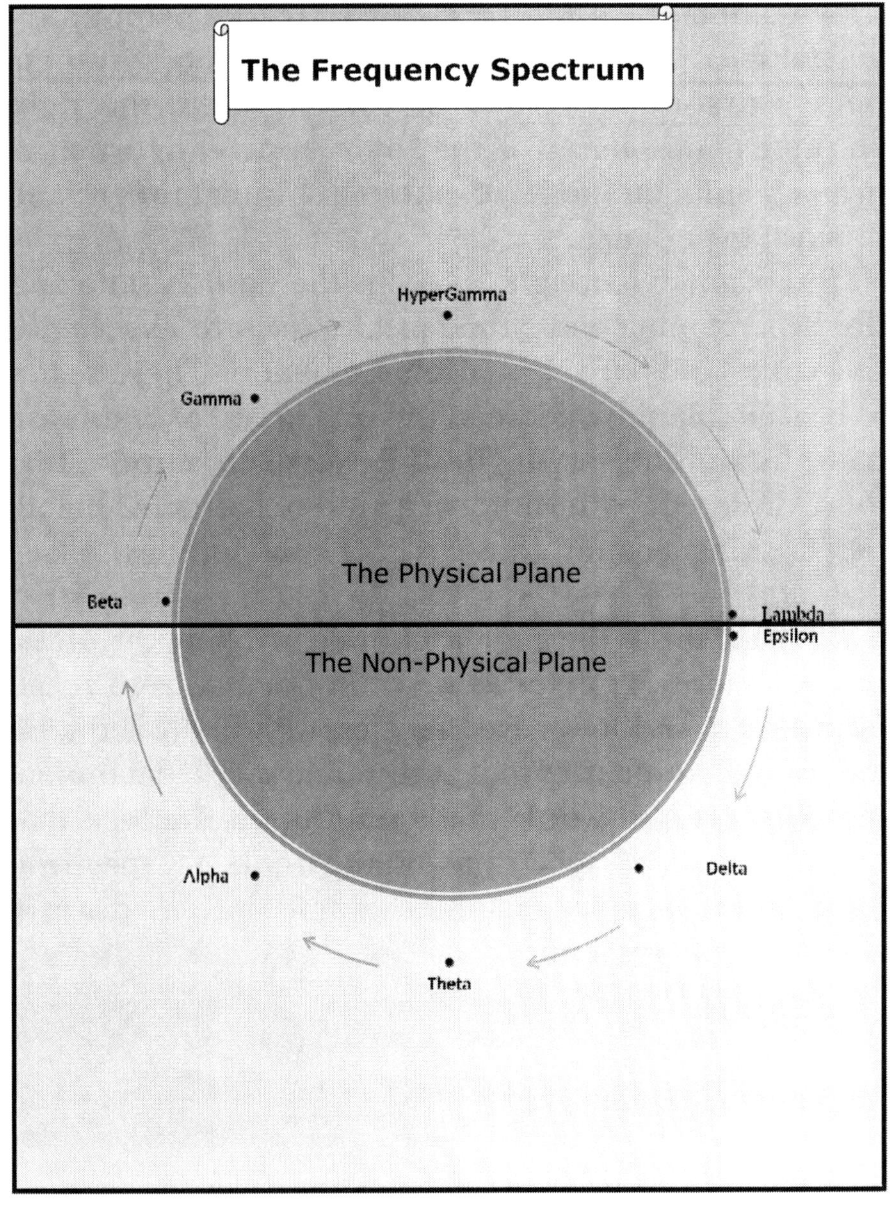
The Frequency Spectrum
HyperGamma
Gamma
The Physical Plane
Beta
Lambda
Epsilon
The Non-Physical Plane
Alpha
Delta
Theta

MUSIC AS MEDICINE

One of the most important and powerful elements in the art of death midwifery is the use of music. Music has the power to affect consciousness dramatically, creating space for healing in the perfect form and measure for each individual. Chosen with care, music will lessen anxiety and fear, decrease pain, soften and release emotional blockages, and open the soul, both for those dying and their families. It has a beneficial effect on anyone who enters the room. Music acts as a link, connecting everyone who hears it to its healing energy.

Before considering the choice of music, we must understand that music begins with our own voice. In the art of death midwifery our voice is our most powerful tool. We must develop our speaking voices into deep and resonant finely tuned instruments. We want to focus on the lower part of our range, which is far more comforting and calming than the upper range. When we speak to our patient we want the timbre, pitch, volume, and cadence to spin a soothing, lyrical cocoon around the dying. The expectation is that in preparation for this work we have recorded our voice and listened to it, shaping and tuning it like the powerful instrument it is. We've softened any rough edges or nasal intonations and have moderated any shrill or abrasive qualities so we can consciously create vocal music with the intention to caress and calm.

For this work, we want our voice to be soft and clear, rich, round, warm, and certainly not tinny or strident. It should exude safety and assurance like a calming lullaby. Slipping into a lilting cadence like that of gentle waves lapping the shore is lightly hypnotic and very useful. It helps to set up an internal tempo, imagining the slow ticking of a metronome…1…2…3…4…1…2…3…4. Speaking in time with this internal metronome…softly…. gently…softly…gently…will encourage one who is anxious or distressed to relax.

Remember the dying can hear, often rather acutely, so never is there a need to be loud. In this culture we tend to underestimate the power of softness and gentleness, but think of the power of a quiet brook upon the rocks. That gentle stream will wear away the rocks rough edges. Your voice can be used to build a strong bridge to the unseen world for the ones you serve.

Ideally, we would have live music at the bedside of the dying. Nothing is more powerful than the living vibrations generated by bedside musicians and singers. There are musicians, primarily harpists, who are specially trained in music thanatology, the creation of music for the death transition. As the need for this service increases, the field of music thanatology is growing; however a good portable CD player or Ipod will do. To accommodate hospital and nursing home safety regulations, it is easiest for the source of music to be battery powered. Pre-recorded music is better than no music at all.

There is growing research into the use of music as medicine. From my personal experience, both as a professional singer for over 30 years and as a death midwife, I know first hand its ability to aid in healing. Just as medicine must be prescribed with care—the right kind in the right amount at the right time—so must music be chosen with care and discernment.

The right music depends on where the one we serve is on the deathing spectrum. In the earlier phases we might be able to ask the patient his musical preferences and *at that time* those would be the best suited. Familiar tunes, those favorite songs steeped in happy memories, can shift and release emotional blockages that might complicate a smooth transition. They can be an impetus to complete unfinished business. Later on the spectrum those same tunes may become an anchor and actually hamper the transition. We will come back to that idea in a moment.

As the patient progresses along the frequency spectrum to the theta state, a different kind of music is better suited. This music, most often found in the "New Age" sections of music stores, tends to be non-rhythmic and often without a discernable melody. Take note: The entrainment music we use in preparation for our work as death midwives is usually not advisable with the dying. Though there can be exceptions to just a bout any rule, generally, we do not want to entrain the brainwaves of the dying to any particular pattern. We do not *know* where they should be. It is our job to find out where they *are* and match them, not to mechanically shift them. By using this non-rhythmic, unstructured "new age" music, the dying will naturally shift to the optimal frequency.

What is important is that, as death midwives, we must be able to ascertain if the music we have selected is working. There are times when it might need moderation;

perhaps a different music choice is better suited. We need to be flexible and understand that this music is for our charge, not for us. We must be very careful not to foist our preferences upon the one dying, but always honor what that person needs or wants. Even if our charge cannot verbally communicate, with sensitivity we can discern how he is responding to the music and make adjustments until we feel certain the music is serving its intended purpose.

There is a wealth of musical recordings created with the intention to open a space for healing. As death midwives it behooves us to become familiar with a broad range of these offerings. Test them out and see what feels right. You will not need dozens of recordings. That is not to say you can't develop a large library of music to draw from, but only that several well-chosen pieces work well for most people in most situations. From a practical standpoint, if one is using a portable CD player and carrying CDs, having ten or so tried and true choices is easier to manage.

That being said, not each piece of music will work optimally for every patient. This is where the artistry and skill of being a death midwife comes into play. Start by intuiting which piece of music might best suit the individual. Once you have set the volume (making sure it is not too loud), watch how your selection "lands" for the patient. With practice you can discern if the choice is the right prescription and dosage. Be willing to try different music and adjust the volume until it feels right. Sometimes one selection will be good for a start, but as things progress, a change is indicated. Watch your patient for those subtle nuances that let you know a change is needed.

I prefer music without vocals for two reasons. First, while certain vocals may be appropriate in a specific situation, at a certain stage of the process most lyrics become a distraction. Never forget that further along on the deathing spectrum, the patient is journeying back and forth between the seen and the unseen and are doing work of which we are often not aware.

Secondly, we may at times feel guided to add our own voice to the music. Again, the energy of a live voice is so much more powerful than that of a recorded one. Focused and projected to the one dying, our voice can send very strong and healing vibrations to affected parts of the physical body, as well as to the chakras, and the etheric, astral and causal bodies.

Experience has taught me that often simple sounds, such as humming, or rounded vowel sounds, such as "ah," are the most effective. It is important to choose notes in our lower register as, in their very sensitive state, those who are dying may find higher notes jarring and unpleasant. Think of a mother singing lullabies to her infant – her voice soft and low. That is the quality we seek.

Straight tones—those held with no vibrato in the voice—are more focused and precise, and, like gentle lasers, can be used to reach specific parts of the body or to project the sound more deeply into the one transitioning. Vibrato tones (those with a moderate tremolo, the natural wave-like quality a relaxed voice will produce) wash over the dying patient like warm waves, functioning more as an overall balm. Once again, skill and discernment are required. Pay attention to intention.

To practice these two types of sound, record your voice creating an "ah" sound, first with a straight tone, then with vibrato. You can use a candle as a guide.

Sit about six inches from a lighted candle. Start making an "ah" sound any way that feels natural to you and watch what happens to the candle. Does the flame ripple with your sound? If it goes out, relight it. Do this several times without trying to shape the sound in any way. Is there a tremolo (slight warbling) to the sound you are making? Is it round and full or tight and tinny? Is it breathy? At first don't try to control anything. Just notice.

Then begin to bring a shape to the sound. Adjust it in whatever way you need for it to become smoother and more rounded. When you achieve that, without constricting the sound, focus it as if you were bringing it to a point. Watch the candle flame. It should not waver. If it wavers, that tells you that you are not focusing the sound enough. There should be no tremolo, just a pure straight note, and the candle should not waver. That is your straight tone.

Next, start with your straight tone and then consciously relax that focus, letting it soften just enough so that a gentle tremolo naturally unfolds. Do not allow your tone to become breathy or to blow out the candle. That is your vibrato. Keep practicing going from a straight tone to a vibrato until you can create either with ease.

Keep in mind, your aim is not to become a professional singer, but just to master making low, soothing straight and vibrato tones at will. This requires practice, and a tape recorder will be a big help.

Sometimes it is not possible or even helpful to add voice aloud, but we can always use our internal voice. Chanting "Om" or "Shalom" aloud may not be welcome or appropriate in certain environments but, with practice, those universally sacred sounds will work just as well chanted internally.

When we add vocals we must be very familiar with the music so that our improvisations are not discordant. It is better not to tone at all than to bring disharmony into the sacred space. Let the music slowly sink into you as you sit with the dying. In time, you will be comfortable enough with the music to add voice when guided by your higher self.

There are times when we will intuit from the soul level that the dying person needs to hear something, perhaps a reassurance or some kind of guidance. If that is the case, we can improvise certain sung phrases like a mantra, carefully laying them over the recorded music to address the specific need. Be ever watchful that this inspiration comes from our spiritual connection to our charge and not from ego. This is not karaoke for the dying!

As mentioned earlier, there comes a place on the deathing spectrum where favorite music from the transitioning one's past becomes more of an anchor than a comfort, a time when the show tunes, country music or Christmas carols will actually hinder the progress of transformation.

During one Christmas season, I experimented with playing carols and seasonal music for the people I was companioning. Those in the more active stages of dying did not respond well to it. I watched the monitors as their heart rates, blood pressure and respiration rates elevated and their anxiety levels actually increased. When I switched back to the more unstructured, non-rhythmic music, they returned to their previous levels. It was clear that for those very close to their final transition, the reminder of the holiday season with all of its emotional attachments was not soothing, but instead increased their discomfort.

Once I had a patient, a 76 year old woman who was dying of pancreatic cancer at the hospital where she had worked as a nurse for 15 years. She had been married for 50 years to a husband who adored her. He bought lots of recordings of her favorite country western music from Branson, Missouri, but she told him to, "Shut that damned stuff off!" Knowing that, my palliative team told me that she wouldn't want music.

When I entered her room, she was in a barely responsive state. I spoke very quietly to her, introducing myself and saying, "I have some music here designed specifically to create a space for healing. May I play it for you? You do not need to say or do anything. I will watch you closely and see if this music is a help or a hindrance." In the most subtle of ways, she gave me permission, but I got the strong non-verbal message that she was also very wary and wouldn't tolerate anything she didn't want.

I selected a piece of music that is appropriate for people in the active and final states of transition. I could tell by carefully monitoring her physical reaction that it was a bit premature for her. Until very recently she had dealt with a lot of uncontrolled pain. I could sense the residual anxiety and tension from that pain plus whatever other psychological and spiritual issues she was dealing with still plaguing her. In this particular case, I switched to a recording that used entrainment to help her relax. This worked much better for her. Much to the amazement of her husband, she allowed the music to continue. It had the added benefit of helping him to relax and opened the space a bit wider for him to begin the very difficult process of letting her go.

In this case, the country and western music that once brought her so much joy was actually acting as an anchor to this shore when what she needed was to be free to make some preliminary ventures to the other shore in the unseen world. The familiar music was like a hook holding her back, grounding her in the past and adding to her pain. It wasn't music that she objected to, it was the *choice of music* that was inappropriate for the work she needed to do at that time.

There are also times, often right at the very edge of transition, when any type stimulus, including the gentlest and most healing of music, is a distraction. With practice, you will feel when that time comes. Then even the use of the person's name acts as an anchor and should no longer be used. It is vital to realize, acknowledge, and honor those times and situations. When that time comes, let the symphony of silence begin, and remember when it comes to music-as-medicine, there is no one prescription that fits all.

Working with the Families

The bitterest tears shed over graves are for words left unsaid and deeds left undone.

– Harriet Beecher Stowe

Death midwifery focuses on the needs of the dying. We concentrate our focus on the days of transition and the several days past what we call death. In an ideal situation, the family will understand, honor, and join in this focus. In many cases, they will do everything in their power to put their own grief temporarily in the background to join in creating this sacred space for transformation. In so doing, they, too, will be uplifted. When the loved one has fully made this transition, then those left behind can fully begin the difficult work of mourning.

It is not often that we experience the ideal situation regarding families in the hospital setting. In this culture, the reality of death is frequently denied and ignored until events force us to face it. Because people are often unprepared, their worst fears play out on the stage of a terminal diagnosis. Add to that any complicated family dynamics, and the stage is set for a lot of conflict and drama...sometimes of epic proportions.

When a death midwife is invited into a private home, generally the family and the person dying are in some kind of accord and will work together; but that is often not the case in a hospital setting. In that setting it is often best to find time alone with the patient. If during the gathering of background information it is ascertained that the family would be a support in creating sacred space, then an invitation to join might be given. If this is not the case, try to mollify some of the messages the patient may be receiving from family and loved ones that might complicate his transition.

There is no greater pain in this world than the loss of a loved one. Family members and friends are often drowning in a sea of emotional agony. That is completely understandable, but bringing that tremendous sadness and emotional upheaval into the presence of the one dying does a great disservice. Separating from this world is laborious work. Just as a mother giving birth labors strenuously, so does the one transitioning from this life into new life. The parallels and symmetry are not coincidental.

The dying one needs to feel unencumbered to make that transition with grace. In spite of the grief they may be feeling, the greatest gift loved ones can give to the one dying is the assurance that they will be okay. No matter how much they will miss and will always miss the one dying, they *will* be okay.

It is not a matter of denying their great sadness. The dying are not fools. Regardless of appearances, the act of dying does not render them senseless. It is a matter of acknowledging that, even though the heart is breaking from the end of the relationship *in its present form*, the relationship will continue throughout eternity *in a new form.* Those left behind, because they love so much, can encourage the one dying to move into that new life and that new relationship with ease, dignity, and grace.

So many times, their loved one's suffering is so overwhelming that the dying will linger, often in a good deal of emotional, spiritual, or physical pain, because the burdensome grief anchors them to this shore. This is heart-rending to witness. For this reason it is quite common for the dying to wait until they are completely alone on the physical plane to make their transition. It is to spare their loved ones the pain of seeing them die.

Please understand, we are not suggesting that those left behind should deny their sorrow. Grief is a massive undertaking that requires our respect and support. What is asked is that they do their best not to bring that grief into the sacred space created specifically for the dying. The willingness to honor sacred space is a priceless and selfless gift of love that only they can give their loved one.

Whether at home or in a nursing home or hospital environment, the following ritual can be used to help loved ones set aside for a time their personal suffering in order to focus solely on the one who is transitioning:

Ritual for Loved Ones before Entering Sacred Space

People about to enter the sacred space should visualize, as precisely and in as much detail as possible, any grief, anger, resentment, fear, regret, despair, etc., that might keep them from focusing selflessly on the one dying. They should use their imagination to really see it, feel it, and touch it. An image may appear that represents these emotions. Whatever that image is, they must honor it. See it sitting in their upturned hands. Then gently and respectfully place this image onto a chair or table outside the sacred space. Let the image know that it will be safe there and can be picked up again upon leaving the sacred space. When leaving, they can pick it back up or not. It might be that with the calm support of the sacred space, the need for it disappears. There is no right or wrong here, and an individual's emotional reaction may not be the same each time she enters and leaves. In any case, it is suggested that this ritual be done each time loved ones enter the sacred space of the dying.

It helps for the family to honestly and sincerely let the person dying know that, while he will be greatly missed, it is okay to move on; the family will be okay. Resolving any unfinished business between the one dying and family members or friends helps the transformation process. Of course, this cannot be forced upon either party, but it is an ideal situation with the potential for tremendous healing.

When the death midwife has knowledge of unfinished business, she may be able to address these issues while dialoguing with the patient. She might attempt to create a healing dreamwalk (to be discussed in the following section) with the patient where these issues are met and resolved on the soul level. This is a delicate situation and must be handled with care, but it can open a pathway for healing.

We always treat family members with the utmost respect and compassion, understanding that they are doing the best they can in an untenable situation. When outside sacred space, console them by being an empathic and nonjudgmental ear. In many cases their pain is greater than that of the one dying. If an opening for healing occurs, gently take them by the hand and lead them through the door. If not, respect where they are at and go quietly about your business, which is serving the one making his transition.

Death Midwifery Techniques

Though death midwifery is an art of being rather than doing, still there are times when spirit will guide us into certain techniques that will support the dying. No technique will be useful for every person or every situation, and it is up to the death midwife to discern if and when one will be beneficial. In this book, we will consider two techniques given to me by spirit: Gaia breath and Dreamwalking.

The Gaia Breath Technique was given to me as inspiration when communing with an elderly patient in the hospital. He was clearly journeying from this shore to the next. From time to time, he would smile delightedly and wave, obviously seeing things and people that I couldn't. At other times, he became quite unsettled, and I could feel fear and anxiety buffeting him like huge waves. Having already established a deep connection with him, I was inspired to do the following breathing technique, which is sometimes helpful when in the presence of great spiritual or emotional suffering:

1. Consciously inhale deeply for a slow count of four while visualizing that you are drawing off the suffering. Draw it toward your heart chakra, but not into it. It is not necessary to bring it into the chakra to be effective.

2. On the next slow count of four, exhale the suffering down to Mother Earth, to Gaia. Ask that she graciously accept it, recycling and restoring the suffering back to its highest expression.

3. Repeat steps 1 and 2 until the suffering lessens.

4. When the suffering has lessened, fill the void created by slowly inhaling for a count of four while drawing divine light and love down through the crown chakra and into the heart, seeing and feeling the light fill the heart chakra.

5. On the next slow count of four, exhale the divine light and love from your heart chakra and send it to the dying one's heart chakra, seeing it bathed in that brilliant light and endless love.

6. Repeat steps four and five until a sense of peace and serenity is established.

In time, as we grow into very strong, pure conduits, we may choose to inhale the suffering into our own heart chakras to truly feel what the one you serve is feeling, but this **is not a recommended practice until you have several years of experience.** If we take that suffering in before we are ready, it would do us more harm than good so it is prudent to be cautious. It is an advanced practice and is never necessary for this technique to be effective.

Dreamwalking is a guided relaxation and visualization technique based in the principles of hypnotherapy. Though a background in hypnotherapy is useful, it is not necessary. Dreamwalking can be used to create a safe place for the one dying or to help resolve unfinished business. This technique is to be used with persons in the earlier parts of the deathing spectrum when spirit guides you to do so. The person would most likely be in a beta or light alpha state, still conscious to some degree and perhaps verbal. They might be in physical, mental, emotional, or spiritual pain. You should ask permission to use dreamwalking, and it is not suggested for use with those in theta or delta states. When someone is in those states, we should not be attempting to direct their consciousness at all.

Whenever possible, ask the patient what type of scenes he finds peaceful and relaxing – for example being at the beach, resting near a graceful waterfall, walking in the woods, picnicking in a field of wild flowers, etc. You will use that input to help create the dreamwalk.

Voice is the most important tool in this technique. It must be very soft, smooth, gentle, and nearly monotone. Find a lulling cadence that will lead the one being served to the very edge of sleep.

1. Select the appropriate music. It should be deeply relaxing and free form in nature.

2. Give the suggestion that your voice creates all of the effort necessary for the person to deeply relax.

3. Begin by guiding the dying through a relaxation starting from the tips of the toes all the way up to the top of the head. Take time and care to address each part of the body, coaching it to release any tension, worry, doubt, anxiety, fear or resistance from the mind and from the soul. Encourage the patient to allow his breath to open and deepen.

4. Create a relaxing image, such as lying on a beach or feeling like a stick of butter melting in the sun. Any image that conjures penetrating warmth and relaxation is good. Use vivid imagery that involves all of the senses.

5. Once the body is completely relaxed, create another image that will guide the person to an even deeper state of relaxation – floating down a gentle stream, walking down a staircase, or going down in an elevator. Be as imaginative and descriptive as possible. Combine this image with counting from one to ten…very, very slowly so that by the count of ten, the person is at a very deep and profound state of relaxation.

6. From here guide the person to create a scene of his own imagining. It can be a real-life image or one that is purely imaginary – anything that makes him feels completely safe, free from pain, and very happy. Urge him to make it as real as possible using

all of his senses. Give him time to explore and enjoy this safe and happy place as the music plays.

7. Based on your knowledge about the person being served, it can be suggested that either a personal spirit guide or a loved one, either living or not, is present. Suggest to the patient that he converse with this special guide or person, asking questions and getting answers he might need, finishing any necessary business with love and deep gratitude. Give him time to do that as the music plays.

8. When intuition tells you enough time as been given, suggest that it is time to leave this place and this special guide or person for now. Let it be known that this safe place and these guides and friends can be easily accessed at will simply by breathing fully, relaxing deeply, and using the power of his imagination.

9. Guide him back through whatever scenario was created to arrive at this safe place, going very slowly back up the stairs, etc., while counting back from ten to one. Make the suggestion that at the count of one, the person will be back to a normal state of consciousness feeling alert, refreshed, relaxed, peaceful, and very, very comfortable.

Until you are skilled at this technique, it might be a good idea to write out a script for a basic dreamwalk. Over time, you may create several different scripts to be used in various situations. With enough practice, it will be easier to spontaneously improvise individually created dreamwalks.

As always, the one we serve has free will, so these techniques will work to the degree the person allows.

Again, we must never feel driven by the ego to use any technique. Most of the time, we will not use any techniques at all. In most cases they are not appropriate. In every case, we need to listen to intuition and follow its guidance.

"Permission to Die" and "The Good Death"

Here I'd like to address two issues that those in the field of death and dying contend with on a daily basis. These are giving permission to die and the concept of a good death. There are differing opinions in each case, and as we grow in our understanding of this transformative process we call death, our thoughts will most likely evolve regarding each. So I'd like to share my thoughts with you on these two important ideas.

Giving "permission" to die is a topic that has many of my colleagues in the field of death and dying divided. On one side, there are those who feel the idea of companions and guides to the dying granting "permission" to die and enjoining our patients to "go into the light" is the height of arrogance. On the other side are those who have seen and experienced first hand the welcome release and positive shifting of energy that such encouragement often brings. So what is the right thing to do? Is there a right thing or should we do nothing at all? In the art of death midwifery it comes down to intention and intuition.

Admittedly, were we to believe we have the power to bestow permission to die as a Pope would grant his followers a dispensation, it would be arrogant in the extreme. We would be fools, for that power does not reside in us.

We can no more compel someone to "go into the light" than we can walk on water.

What we can and should do is remind and empower those we guide that, when the time is right—and they will know when that time is—they can relax, let go, and flow into the stream of well being. We want to make it very clear that we are reminding them, not telling them. We can assure them that should they see the white light they need not fear it. They can go into that light and embrace it, knowing it is the God/Goddess of their understanding, their highest concept of divine intelligence, and that it is safe to do so. Only they can make the choice to let go or to embrace the light. I believe that at the deepest layers of consciousness we all know what we need to do; we just need to trust and remember. The death midwife helps his charge to remember. In this case, the intention is a benediction.

Ideally this encouragement should come from family and loved ones first. If they cannot do that for whatever reasons, the death midwife can. Even if the family and loved ones are able to give that encouragement, the death midwife can support them by repeating the reminder at the appropriate moment.

This type of reminder should not be given by rote, nor should it be given unless or until the one dying is near the part of the deathing spectrum just before crossing over into the unseen world. Timing the reminder properly is crucial. To give it earlier in the spectrum might very well distress rather than empower. We would never want to give the dying the impression that we were trying to move them along, a "Here's your hat, what's your hurry," type of thing. That would be an act of violence. One should transcend ego and rely on the divine urge so that the reminder comes at the right time.

So in the art of death midwifery we do not grant permission to die nor command our charge to go into the light. With great respect and compassion we remind and empower our brothers and sisters who may have forgotten just who and what they are.

Next, let us consider the concept of a "good death." Certainly, if we had the power, we would wave a magic wand to ensure that every person's transition from this life to the next life be peaceful and pain free, without struggle or suffering of any kind. We do not have that power. With the advances in hospice and palliative care, a peaceful, pain-free death has become the gold standard and is, to varying extents, possible to achieve; however, no matter what advances medicine makes, there will still be suffering. No matter what advances psychology makes, there will still be suffering. It may be, as some spiritual traditions suggest, that suffering is the nature of life on this material plane. It may be that a certain kind of suffering is necessary for our soul's growth. It may be that some suffering is an essential part of our patient's journey. We are not in a position to know with certainty what a good death is for any given soul, and fooling ourselves into thinking we do know is arrogant and unhelpful.

That desire to make death conform to our notion of what is "good" is the ego refusing to surrender to God, the small self thinking it knows better than the Infinite what should transpire. It is an easy trap to fall into, and we must guard against it at all times. Our task as death midwives is to become comfortable with the paradox that, while we wish for all suffering to cease, we nevertheless understand that at times, suffering, in some kind, may be in divine right order, beyond our present ability to comprehend.

Being individualized facets of God, our lives and our paths are uniquely ours. We never really know what another has come to this life to learn or the manner in which he will learn it. As difficult as it can be for a compassionate death midwife to bear, there will be times when what we witness will not seem to be a "good death" at all.

Remember, all we are required to do is to create sacred space, direct and focus divine light and love to those we serve, surround them with unconditional love and acceptance, and then bear witness to what transpires. We are not responsible for their journey. We act merely as guides and witnesses. That is all we can do…and if we do it well…it is enough…it is far more than enough.

Bearing Witness in the Garden of Gethsemane

No one knows whether death, which people fear to be the greatest evil, may not be the greatest good.

– Plato

Perhaps the most difficult and challenging situation a death midwife will encounter is bearing witness in the Garden of Gethsemane. This is the phrase I use to describe communing with a dying person who is trapped in extraordinary suffering, be it physical, mental, emotional, spiritual or a combination thereof. It is an anguish that nothing and no one can touch for reasons that often are solely between that person and the God/Goddess of his understanding. Being a container for this degree of suffering is the ultimate test for a death midwife. It can bring us to our knees if we are not strongly rooted in spirit. If we are unable to bear the tension of this challenge, it is better to acknowledge that limitation and, rather than contribute one iota to the suffering, remove ourselves from the sacred space. If we can keep sacred space open to allow and support the Garden of Gethsemane patient in doing what needs be done, without judgment or flinching, we offer one of the greatest gifts a human can give to another.

It is more likely that we will walk the Garden with people dying in the hospital. In the hospital, the physical suffering can be complicated by resistance by either the patient or family members to the shift from active treatment to comfort measures only. When the physical condition deteriorates to the point where death is the only real conclusion, the medical staff will often suggest the patient be put on "comfort measures only." This means that artificial means of continuing life beyond its normal scope are eliminated and only those medicines and procedures that contribute to comfort will be maintained.

Until the decision to embrace comfort measures only is made, the patient will be subjected to forced feedings, blood tests and other uncomfortable procedures, while the medical staff is limited in just how effectively they can manage pain. In a terminal situation, the dosages of pain medicines required to eliminate suffering will sometimes inhibit respiration, slowing it, at times to the point of ceasing it altogether. Making the decision to accept comfort measures only is often and very understandably a difficult and painful one for the family.

Sometimes, the patient or family may be in denial and unable to acknowledge that death is near. Sometimes the family harbors the erroneous and guilt-ridden idea that by choosing comfort measures only they are "killing" their loved one. This is completely untrue and yet many families struggle with that decision because of this notion. On some occasions there are less than selfless motivations on the part of family members to keep the patient alive, as matters of wills and inheritance loom large. Sometimes, the patient himself may have heroic intentions of staying alive just a little longer—often so as not to abandon his family.

"Mr. Smith" was a 51-year-old man with renal and respiratory failure. He had a tracheotomy, decubitus ulcers everywhere, and a huge open wound on his abdomen, so deep as to expose muscle. He was nearly a quadriplegic. A recipient of a kidney transplant that ultimately failed, he and his wife were in litigation over what they believed was malpractice. The doctors felt he couldn't survive, but he wanted everything possible done to keep him alive until the lawsuit was resolved. Before he could feel free to move on, he wanted to know his wife was provided for. He was, quite simply, in hell.

Never have I witnessed so much physical suffering. Because he wanted to be kept alive at all costs, the medical team was limited in what it could do to manage his pain. When I first met him, he was in the midst of dialysis, panicked and struggling to breathe and terribly frustrated because his tracheotomy left him unable to communicate.

This was not an ideal situation in which to create sacred space. There were two dialysis technicians in the room carrying on personal conversations, and everywhere were chaos and clutter that I could do nothing to improve. Part of me wanted to give up, but I just couldn't leave this man who was so obviously suffering.

Choosing a piece of music that felt appropriate, I focused on becoming a conduit to infuse that place of confusion and pain with peace. While the effect wasn't 100% successful, things did shift somewhat. The first improvement was that the technicians moved into a far corner and spoke in hushed tones. Mr. Smith's blood pressure and respiration slowed a bit, and there were even times when it looked like he might relax and doze a little. However each time he began to let go and fall asleep, he'd yank himself back up. His fear was palpable: if he allowed himself to lose consciousness, he would never regain it.

I sat with him, lightly touching the one small place on his arm where there were no wounds and allowing divine energy to flow to him. All of a sudden there was a suffusion of golden light, and I felt an intense surge of energy flow from the top of my head to the tips of my toes. It was so strong it was almost scary, but I just relaxed and let it flow through me. Carefully watching Mr. Smith, I saw the energy flow into him. His eyes rolled back into his head in a rhythmic pattern, back, back, back, lasting the entire time I felt the flow in my own body. When the flow left me, his eyes settled back to normal, and the golden wash of color gently faded. Though not relaxed, he seemed a bit more comfortable.

The second time I visited Mr. Smith, he was not having dialysis, and I hoped things would be a bit calmer for us. For the first hour it was, though it was still very apparent that his suffering was immense. When the nurse came in to do his dressing change, she asked if I would stay with him while she did this very painful work.

His suffering defied words. There was virtually no place on this man's body that wasn't a gaping wound, exposing muscle and sinew. It took over two hours to clean and change the dressings, and this was done twice a day, every day. The abdominal wound went almost all the way through to his organs, and the wounds on his back were worse. The tracheotomy was the only thing that kept us from hearing him scream. I, however, could feel him screaming in every cell of my body. I wanted to scream with him.

I didn't, of course. Instead, I held him where I could and softly told him to focus on me and the music, assuring him that I wouldn't let him fall, for surely he was teetering on the precipice of endurance. This routine of torture was performed daily, and I was awed by his perseverance, his willingness to suffer this agony for his wife.

When the nurse finished, I stayed with him. He let me know he wanted the doctor. He wanted more pain medication. I told his nurse, and she said she would bring some. Thirty painful minutes later there was still no medication. I then called the palliative care team, and they made sure Mr. Smith got his meds. The team's nurse spoke with him. He knew his situation was hopeless yet he wanted everything done to stay alive no matter how much he suffered. He indicated that he was not afraid of dying. My sense was he felt that if he could just last long enough for a financial settlement to his lawsuit, he would feel he had provided for his wife and could then die in peace.

Though the palliative care team was able to manage his pain to a degree, because he refused comfort measures only, they were limited. He was willing to suffer this pain for his family. The very least I could do was support him and bear witness to his suffering. It did not eliminate his agony, but it eased his mind a bit to know someone was there to help him endure it, to know that there was someone who wouldn't run from it.

To bear witness in the Garden of Gethsemane is an opportunity to learn true humility. To be in the presence of such intense suffering, to companion one in that moment while remaining present with extreme pain knowing we are helpless to relieve it, is a truly humbling experience. It can bring us to our knees in either torment or in surrender. If we can surrender to the experience, the door to transformation may open. Beyond the thorns, flowers bloom in the Garden of Gethsemane.

ETHICS

When we bear witness to another's transition from this life to new life we are being granted an extreme privilege. It is our responsibility to handle this privilege with the highest of ethics. While it is beyond the range of this book to explore all of the ethical considerations in depth, we will mention the keystones of conduct and encourage anyone wishing to serve as death midwives to honor the strictest code of responsible behavior. Hospitals, hospices, and nursing homes generally have trainings you will be expected to complete before being allowed to serve. Each will go more into depth on its particular code of standards, confidentiality policies, and HIPAA regulations; but, regardless of whether you serve in a public or private setting, certain rules apply.

First and foremost is respect. Respect for the one you serve and her family. With all the invasions of personal space that those dying must suffer, dignity can often be compromised. It is, therefore, one of our most sacred charges to accord the dying with the dignity someone making this most sacred of transitions is due. Show respect and accord them the same dignity that you would a revered teacher, for that is what they will become.

This involves things such as making sure that they are properly covered and that the bedclothes are orderly. We must be sure that we touch respectfully and in neutral places that will not cause discomfort. Always ask permission before touching, and always be courteous and polite. Details are important. Everything we do matters so we are never careless in the presence of the dying. Remember, too, that no matter how the family may be reacting at the time, they also deserve respect. Death brings out the best and the worst in people so we need to be compassionate to everyone involved.

In addition to guarding the dignity of the dying, we must guard their privacy. What we see and hear is sacred and we should treat it as would a priest in a confessional. Confidentiality is the law both morally and legally. The relationship with the one we serve is often very intimate, and that trust should never be violated. Hospitals, hospices, and nursing homes have strict guidelines safeguarding confidentiality, and breaching them would be cause for dismissal—and in some cases criminal prosecution. In a private home situation it should be no different. We can never be cavalier in the treatment of our charge's personal information.

Health and hygiene is of the utmost importance. We always wash our hands before entering and after leaving the sacred space of the dying. It is advisable to wipe down any equipment, such as portable musical devices, carrying cases, etc. after each patient. The immune systems of the dying are quite fragile, and we would never want to complicate their situation by bringing germs or viruses into their environment.

Our personal hygiene is supremely important. Be freshly bathed and shampooed on the day of service. Nails should be well groomed and kept fairly short.

Jewelry should be kept to a minimum. Do not use fragrances as the dying's senses are quite acute, and fragrances can be very annoying. Use unscented deodorant and keep breath mints on hand. Wear simple clothing and shoes that are comfortable and clean. Professionalism, courtesy, respect, and good hygiene are expected of the death midwife. The dying deserve our very best…always…and in all ways.

THE DYING ARE OUR TEACHERS

Our best teachers are our patients. They will tell us what they need. Our patients' responses, however subtle, will give us a sense of where they are in their journey and how best we can support them. We must be humble enough to understand that we will never finish learning about this mysterious transition called death. We will never become experts. Each person we guide will be unique and will teach us different things. Each death we attend will change us, and the learning will deepen. We can never become set in our ways; the dying will always present new challenges and lessons, will grant us new insights and allow us to witness miracles.

Our time spent with the dying will shape, inform, and enlighten us. If we fully embrace the experience, residing in the liminal space between worlds can transform us. We will come away knowing that no matter what we think we give, we receive a thousand-fold more in return.

The following are several stories of people I had the honor to commune with over the years:

In 1992, "Mr. Jones" lived alone in the desert outside of Phoenix, Arizona. His wife had died a couple of years prior. He was now in the end stages of terminal lung cancer. His friends took turns checking in on him and the daughter from whom he had been estranged was, in the final days, trying to make a connection. As a new hospice employee, I cared for him in twelve hours shifts three times a week.

In the beginning, he could carry on conversations. He told me that he was saving up enough pain medications to end his life when he decided it was too much for him. He asked me if I had ever read, "Final Exit" by Derek Humphry. Humphry at the time was the head of the Hemlock Society; a group dedicated to the right of self-deliverance and assisted suicide. Assisted suicide was then, and is still today, a highly controversial subject. He watched my reaction to his question. I told him that I had indeed read the book. He asked my opinion. I told him that I felt each person's death was unique, and that I could not ever judge another's choice.

He tested me over the next couple of days, trying to sense whether I meant what I had said. I did; if he chose to end his life when the suffering became too much for him to bear, I would honor his choice. I would not participate in his choice, but I would honor it. My non-judgmental attitude opened a safe space for him. Trusting that there was unconditional love and acceptance from me seemed to make all the difference to him, and he never mentioned it again. He did not choose to end his life.

He had two small dogs that loved him dearly. They sat up on the couch with him, standing guard. They were very protective of him and made washing and feeding him more than a little challenging. They cuddled up with him, licking and licking as if they were trying to lick him back to health.

Days turned into weeks while he lingered, now unable to speak. His friends began to wonder what was keeping him on this earth since he wanted so badly to join his beloved wife. They gave me a video of his wedding, and asked me to play it for him.

I played it over and over for hours and hours...the refrains from favorite songs, the laughter and celebration created a hypnotic reverie. At one point I was urged to begin a dialogue with his departed wife. "Mary," I said, "your husband is laboring to birth himself into new life. Can you help guide and ease his way?" The air thickened with a gooey dense feeling. Then the dogs started barking wildly, jumped off the couch, and stood looking up into the darkened loft, wagging their tales as if welcoming an old friend.

Animals have far more finely tuned senses than we do. There was no doubt in my mind that they could see something or someone I couldn't. I felt very clearly that Mary was there to help ease her husband's passage, though that would not be for a few more days.

A day later as he lay on the couch in obvious distress, I committed the error, mentioned earlier, of ***telling*** Mr. Jones that he should go "into the light." Not only was that an act of arrogance, in this very special case, it was physically painful for him as well. He lived in the middle of the desert with all of his windows fully covered in black out curtains. I assumed that was to keep out the heat of summer. Wrong. What I came to understand later from his friends was that he was a former pilot who got severe migraines from sunlight. No matter how well intentioned my telling him to go into the light might have been, it caused him physical pain to even visualize light. He let me know that in no uncertain terms too.

His telling me to "F*** off!" after so many days with of being "unresponsive," was a Zen stick lesson well taught. The dying have no time for "niceiosity"- those phony affectations that serve as social lubricant in our society. "Niceiosity is not a spiritual virtue," my spiritual mentor reminds me often, and the dying certainly have no inclination toward it.

Needless to say, I was mortified. Who did I think I was? What had I done to this poor man? I apologized to Mr. Jones, asked his forgiveness, and never made that mistake again.

He died shortly thereafter. I was not with him at the time. Unfortunately, his anguished daughter did not honor the "Do Not Resuscitate" order, which is standard with all hospice patients. She did not follow procedures and call hospice when her father died, but rather called 911. Instead of her father's transition being one of dignity and peace, it was filled with trauma and chaos. Paramedics are required to do everything medically possible to resuscitate a dead or dying person, so Mr. Jones was subjected to shocking heart defibrillation paddles and other heroic measures to bring him back to life. As we'll discuss in a later chapter, what we do to the body during and even after crossing the deathing threshold, affects the soul's journey. This unfortunate and unwanted intervention unnecessarily complicated Mr. Jones's transition.

Mr. Jones taught me humility and the healing power of unconditional love and acceptance. His dogs taught me that animals have an uncanny ability to know when their guardians are dying and can often sense those in the non-physical more easily than we can. His daughter taught me the importance of making our final wishes known clearly and emphatically to all involved so they will be respected when the time comes.

My father was the first of my parents to die. In 1998, it was his diagnosis of biliary cancer that led me to become trained as a hospice home health care provider. As his condition deteriorated, I knew he would need my ability to physically care for him.

Dad was a very strong, hardworking Greek man, a restaurateur and self-made millionaire without a high school diploma. Growing up in the mean streets of depression-era Chicago, he was very tough. He'd left school at the age of 15 to help support his family and was delivering flowers a block away when the Valentine's Day Massacre happened. He could hear the machine gun fire. He never cried when his mother and four siblings died. He didn't use Novocain when having a cavity drilled or pain medication when passing kidney stones. Did I say tough? He was tough with a capital "T."

Matters were complicated by my family's unwillingness to accept that he had cancer. He was 83 years old and exploratory surgery to confirm it 100% was too risky. He didn't want it, anyway. Being the only one in the family to accept what was happening, I became a lightening rod for my family's anger and despair. Having experienced that working with other hospice clients, it was not completely unexpected. Often the care provider is a safe place to dump all those dark emotions, and we learn not to take it personally. With my own family, of course, it was harder.

Several times I asked my father if he wanted me to leave upper state New York where I lived and come back to Florida to care for him. My offers were bluntly rebuked. Finally, six weeks before my father's death, my mother, in her late 70s and having health issues of her own, became too physically and emotionally frail to care for him alone. Begrudgingly, my father allowed me to put my job on hold and spend the last weeks of his life caring for him and my mother.

It was his desire to die at home, and he was getting ready to do so. The anchor was my mother. They had been married for 45 years. Over and over she would tell him that he was her best friend and couldn't leave her, that she couldn't manage without him. So he held on in what had to have been tremendous pain, though he would not acknowledge it. This was, after all, the man who didn't use pain medication. As the pain grew too much for even him to bear, my father let me massage his back several times a day trying to relieve it. He was tired of it all—the many minor surgeries due to the biliary drain placed in his side, all the hospitalizations due to the complications from the drain, all the weight loss of sixty pounds and counting. He was tired, wanted to die, and told us so in those exact words.

"Don't say that!" my mother cried. "I couldn't take it if you died."

Because of my mother's denial, I was not able to get hospice in to help my father until the last few days of his life. By then, his pain was so bad that he agreed to take morphine by mouth. The only way my mother would allow hospice into their home was on the promise that they would never mention the word "hospice" in my father's presence. She pretended that he didn't know what his condition was or what was going on as if by not mentioning the word she could keep this from happening. This form of magical thinking is common among those who will be left behind and it is heart-wrenching to witness.

As much as I hated the pretense, I went along with it for my mother's sake. Clearly, she needed this charade. One day the phone rang, and my father picked it up. "It's hospice wanting to talk to you," he said handing me the phone. You cannot fool the dying, and it is insulting to try.

Weeks before, I had the premonition that the day my father died would begin with me awakened in the dark hours of early morning by my mother shouting from the other side of the house, "Joellyn! Joellyn, wake up!" That is precisely what happened on the morning of September 4, 1998.

My father, who had never vomited in his life, was throwing up blood. The pain got ahead of him, and we now needed a stronger liquid form of morphine. I called the hospice nurse and told her what was going on. She said, "Your father is bleeding out." She wasn't going to be able to come to our house for several hours but ordered liquid morphine to be delivered immediately.

"This is the worst day so far," my father said to me as I washed his emaciated body.

"You can't die, Harry," my mother told him, "You're my best friend."

"If I'm your best friend, I'll die today," he told her. And that is exactly what he did.

As time went on and my father worsened, my mother started to panic. She wanted to call an ambulance to take him to the hospital. There was no way I would let that happen. My father wished to die at home, and I would make sure he his wish was honored.

I did my best to calm my mother down and get her to eat a little something. At one point, just before three o'clock in the afternoon, I left my father's side for a brief moment. When I returned, he had gotten himself out of bed and was standing up staring into space. Just staring with the most amazing, wondrous look on his face, as if seeing a beautiful scene before him, and I believe he actually did.

"Oh…no," was all I could manage with tears straining my voice but it was enough to draw my mother back into his room.

A whisper of a smile crossed his face and then I watched the life drain out of him. He withered and crumpled like a flower left out in the sun without water. His mouth moved as if trying to say something but no sound came out.

I supported and guided him to a chair against the wall and put my hand on his heart. My mother and I told him that we loved him. I thanked him for taking care of our family all these many years, and I promised him I'd take care of mom. And then…his heart slowed…and…ever so gently…stopped. We stayed that way, my mother, my father and I, frozen in a still-life portrait, until an hour later when the hospice nurse arrived.

The nurse and I carried my father to his bed and dressed him in the clothes my mother had chosen for him to wear. Because of all the internal bleeding, I needed to lift his head up and to the side so the blood that kept filling his body cavity could drain into a basin. Once, twice, three, four, five times…I was so very glad my mother was no longer in the room. My father, being my mother's best friend, kept his word to her, like he always did.

The next morning, I was drawn to the family room by an inhuman wailing. It was the keening of a wild animal with its paw caught in a trap, and it sent chills down my spine. It was my mother. At that moment I heard my mother die. Oh, she didn't die physically that day. It took her body four years to actually follow; but her heart died with my father, and she was never the same after that.

From my father's death I learned that one can die with strength and dignity. I witnessed the power of will we have even in the timing of our leave taking, and I learned that a best friend can die of a broken heart.

My mother's death was a slow and protracted one that began in earnest on September 4, 1998. Over the next four and a half years she changed from a strong, gutsy woman into a frail and frightened one. Her health began to decline; first her kidneys failed, then her heart. I brought her home to live with my husband and me for the last ten months of her life. She needed care twenty-four hours a day, seven days a week and I was the one best prepared to give that to her.

Dialysis for a frail 81 year old was a nightmare. The staff was not trained or prepared for a patient that needed individualized care that fell out of the normally proscribed treatment plan as my mother did. She suffered greatly from the many complications and surgeries resulting from the dialysis. She grew weak, and, because her pride made her eschew a walker, falls became a real problem. She took several bad ones before we could finally convince her to use one. "If you break a bone in your state, I'm afraid it will kill you," I told her.

My mother began to see people and things we could not. She saw a man clothed in a black robe who stood at the base of her bed, offering her a gift wrapped in gold. She saw a little white dog…

A few years prior, my parents had made the decision to put down the little white toy poodle they'd had for many years. My mother loved Twiggy with all her heart. She suffered a small stroke when Twiggy was put down and was devastated by her loss. It is my belief that Twiggy, though my mother never mentioned her by name, came to help ease my mother's terror of dying and guide her into a new life. The little white dog appeared from time to time, soothing my mother each time it did.

My mother reached the point where she just didn't want to go through any more dialysis, any more surgeries, any more anything, yet she still had a great fear of death. She would wait for me to set her up in her chair, feed her, get her cleaned up, dressed and ready to watch television before going out to run errands and such. One day I had not been out of the house for five minutes when my cell phone rang. It was my mother. She'd fallen and couldn't get up. Turning the car around, I rushed home.

"What were you doing?" I asked.

"I wanted to go to the bathroom," she said.

"Before I left I asked if you needed to and you said no."

"Well, I didn't want you bothering with me. I can do it myself."

"I see that," I replied, lifting her from the floor and helping her to the bathroom.

Trying to protect my mother's privacy, I urged, "Please, take as much time as you need. I'll be right across the hall in the office. When you're ready, call me and I'll help you get back to the couch and settled in."

"All right," she answered.

Several minutes went by and the next thing I heard was a crash and a groan. I flew the few feet from my desk to the bathroom and found my mother lying in a heap on the rim of the bathtub, her hand gashed open to the bone and bleeding badly.

"Why didn't you call me?" I cried, starting to panic from all the blood.

"I can do it myself," she insisted, as I called 911.

By this time, 911 knew us by name. In the previous ten months we'd called more than a dozen times. Minutes later when the paramedics arrived they bandaged her hand and got her onto the gurney for another ride to the emergency room. Moving her caused a lot of pain in her side, and I started to really worry.

Her nephrologist, a very good and caring doctor, met us at the emergency room. After examining my mother, she confirmed my worst fears. My mother had cracked her ribs in the fall. Ten months of sleep deprivation and worry climaxed as I crumpled into tears, sure that this meant my mother's death was looming. I admit to wondering just how much of this was an accident and how much was my mother's attempt to take back some control over her own life…and death.

With the help of a very dear friend, we got my mother to one more dialysis treatment, but it was clear the staff couldn't handle a woman with cracked ribs; and the pain of getting there was too much for her. In the language of mothers and daughters she let me know that she had had enough. She was near the end of what she could endure.

The Friday before her death I got her up and onto the couch for her morning meds and breakfast as I always did. She had no appetite and didn't really want to take the meds. I nudged the milk shake she usually enjoyed closer, gently prodding her to sip some.

"You push me too much," she mumbled.

"What?" I asked startled, realizing the inevitable shift was beginning.

"You push me too much," she said again, softly and sadly.

Dropping to my knees to be eye level with her, I whispered, "Okay, mom, I won't push you any more. What would you like me to do?

She didn't say another word. She just began petting the little white dog while I started making calls.

I always regretted that with all the stress of my father's death, I didn't get the call out to my brothers soon enough for them to be at his side when he died. That was not going to happen again. Two of my brothers came that Friday to vigil with my husband and me until the end. The decision was made that day to remove my mother from dialysis and bring hospice into the home.

It is my feeling that we die very much in the manner we lived. My mother was a complex and often difficult person, and her death was very complex and difficult. From that Friday until Sunday morning when she died, she labored hard and long to birth herself into her next life. Much of that labor was due to her tremendous fear of death, her conviction that she was going to hell. Some of the struggle was, I feel, due to unfinished business.

My brothers, husband, and I did all that we could to alleviate her fear, to help tie up what loose ends we could, but still she lingered. We felt helpless and frustrated as we took turns staying up; making sure someone was with her twenty-four hours a day to administer morphine and bearing witness to untenable spiritual and emotional suffering.

On Sunday morning, January 19, 2003, one of my brothers brought in a video of his oldest son and him skiing in Japan. My nephew, having mustanged his way into Annapolis, is a lieutenant commander in the Navy. My mother was very proud of him, and they were extremely close. When my nephew left for a two-year stint in Japan, my mother's health was already failing, and the chances of her still being alive when he returned was growing slim.

"Don't go anywhere, Grandma," he told her, "Just don't go anywhere."

"I'll try," she answered. And she did. She really did.

My brother popped in the video and pointed out all the scenes to my mother. He joked and shared stories of his Christmas in Japan with his son, entertaining her in the way only he could.

I came out to join them, sitting on the other side of my mother, the three of us watching my nephew fly down the steep slope. Gradually, I realized that the muscle twitches that plagued my mother had slowed and then stopped. Her arm finally still. Then I looked at her face, eyes open gazing at her beloved grandson, a small bit of drool running down the corner of her mouth, so still…and quiet. She was gone. She died seeing her grandson for the last time, and I believe that was what she had waited for…just to see him one… more…time.

From my mother's death I learned the value of having someone outside the family dynamic create and hold sacred space. It is a Herculean task for a loved one to achieve and maintain that balance. It is too hard for someone providing 24/7 care to have the strength to be that container and conduit. I wish we could have had a death midwife present for my mother's transition. Her death was the catalyst to train others so that any who choose may have those services available.

"Sandy" was a young dancer and dear friend of mine. We'd done several musicals together in Florida. He was only 21 when he was diagnosed with AIDS. This was before my initiation into the path of death midwifery, and I had no real experience with death, especially the imminent death of one so young. He came to spend some time with me, staying for a week or so. While in his presence, I realized how much we diminish death in this culture, how casually we bandy it about in our language with no real sense of what it is.

"Oh, these shoes kill me."
"I'm so embarrassed I could die."
"We died laughing."
"I could kill her!"
"My boss is working me to death."

I caught myself, in the presence of one so close to death's actuality, thoughtlessly trivializing it with inane and commonplace expressions. The realization of just how disrespectful and ignorant I was being was like a slap in my face.

Sandy had to end his stay with me early. His health was declining fast. He had infection after infection, and thrush coated his throat. He called to tell me he was going back home to California to be with family.

Later he called from the hospital and told me how terrified he was of death, how angry he was to be 21 and dying. I didn't know what to say or do. He'd write, and I'd write back; but I became afraid to call him. It was with Sandy that I discovered the superstition of magical thinking and how we, who would like to deny death, fall prey to it. *If I don't call him, he won't die. If I don't pick up the phone, everything will be okay.* Well, he did and it wasn't. His former partner called to tell me Sandy had died…alone in the hospital, screaming at the top of his lungs.

Sandy taught me that there is no magic in magical thinking; there is only regret. I learned that for some, screaming at the injustice of death may not be a "good" death for those witnessing it, but it can be the "right" death for some who die that way.

"Spice" was another wonderful dancer and dear friend of mine. He was Cuban with a dynamic personality, and he faced his AIDS diagnosis head on, fearlessly, unwilling to give up without a fight. That was his way. He was a fighter so for him fighting was the natural way to meet this challenge. At the time I was living in New York City, and I'd see him when he flew up from Florida to see top HIV/AIDS specialists. Eventually, though, his condition deteriorated to the point where he was too sick to travel. Then just before his 38th birthday, I got a call.

"I want you to come to Florida to visit me."

"Spice, I don't have money for a plane ticket. I don't think I can."

"You have to. I need to see you. I'm waiting for you, and I don't have a lot of time." Spice never took no for an answer.

"All right. I'll figure out something, and be there in a couple of days. Can you wait that long?"

"Just hurry," he said and hung up. I did.

I got there a couple of days later and was stunned by what I saw. My strong, vibrant friend had wasted down to about 85 pounds and lost most of his hair. He looked like a mummy, shrunken, dry, so very weak and hurting everywhere.

I sat on the couch with him and very gently took his feet onto my lap. Those talented feet, which had danced in so many shows, were now just bruised bones scraping against each other. He wanted me to massage them, so that is what I did, gently, thoroughly, infusing my touch with all the love in my heart. His sighs of pleasure and relief brought me to tears. Back then many people didn't like to touch people with AIDS, so this simple massage, this loving touch, was to him, a great gift. It was something so very simple, yet it mattered so much.

I massaged and massaged, kneading those tender feet as long as he wanted, and I could see his whole body relax. That simple quiet time on the couch with my dear friend is a memory I treasure.

The next day Spice wanted to take his partner and me out to Sunday brunch. It also happened to be the day he went blind; but that didn't stop Spice.

We arrived at the restaurant with Spice so weak he was now in a wheelchair. As we were escorted to our table people stopped eating and stared. He was so emaciated and withered that his appearance was startling. I caught the pain in his partner's face; we were both glad Spice couldn't see their expressions.

We did out best to keep the conversation light, but it was obvious that this outing was exhausting what little strength Spice had left. We put tiny teaspoons of food on his plate, telling him what he'd find at noon, at 3 o'clock, at 6 o'clock, but he ate nothing. It was all he could do to keep his head up. We finished quickly and left. The hostess was so kind; she didn't charge for Spice's uneaten brunch.

We got him home and into bed. I told him I had to leave the next day. He smiled and told me he loved me. "I love you too," I said. Then he closed his eyes and went into a very deep sleep.

After several hours of watching my sweet friend, I etched his face into my memory, then kissed him lightly on the cheek and left, flying back to New York City on Monday.

On Tuesday, a good friend of Spice's called to let me know he had died a few hours prior. He'd awakened from that deep sleep I'd left him in bleeding out. He was very aware of what was happening and was determined to go out on his own terms. He shouted out orders to his caretakers right until the final second. That was Spice, always in charge and always strong.

From Spice I learned that the dying can, indeed, wait to say goodbye if that is what they need. He also taught me the value of loving, respectful touch. And grace….

In the hospital, I had a patient who was actively dying. Because she was so very near the threshold we call death, it was clear that she didn't need or want touch, music, or any stimulation at all. I respected that and sat in silence with her, maintaining sacred space and bearing witness. However, as I was leaving, I stood up and telepathically encouraged her to continue to gather her energy toward her crown chakra to facilitate the withdrawal of consciousness from that center. I very gently ran my hand through her subtle fields about 10 inches from the top of her head.

Stunning me, she immediately curled into a fetal position. At that moment in the spectrum of death, even a movement through her auric field was too much for her to bear.

This woman taught me that the dying are sometimes even more sensitive and responsive than I had realized.

From another woman in the hospital I learned that we can sense and feel the drawing up of consciousness, of life force, toward the crown chakra during the deathing process. In the eastern traditions, having the life force exit from the highest chakra, the crown chakra, is considered the most desirable situation, though it may exit from any of the chakras. According to this tradition, exiting from the highest chakra possible is most propitious for the soul's next incarnation.

As a spiritual scientist, it matters not what various traditions dictate but rather what one's own experience suggests. My time with the dying suggests that indeed, consciousness, the soul, life force, whatever we call it, rises upwards towards the head as we come closer to death. With practice, it can be sensed.

How one senses that drawing up will be different depending on each individual's unique way of recognizing energy. For me, it is an awareness of warmth as the life force draws towards the top of the head, while simultaneously feeling coolness pool below. Where I feel the boundary of warmth and coolness indicates the place in the body where the life force currently gathers and, potentially, from which chakra it might exit. We can then suggest to the ones we serve that they focus their attention to the top of their head, allowing their spirit to leave the body from that chakra.

From spending many hours in intimate communion with the dying, I've noticed certain phenomena. With a good deal of time spent in silence and witnessing, the ability to see auric fields develops or expands. In addition, when a person is very close to crossing the threshold we call death, a different set of eyes, astral eyes, may appear. These eyes, which appear to me often superimposed upon the closed eyelids of the person I am with, are of a color not seen in normal human eyes. These eyes tend to be a silver color or sometimes like the color of clear water. They will look directly at me, wide open and seemingly devoid of any emotion. While I cannot say with certainty what they are or what they represent, my best thought is that these are the eyes of the higher self, the soul, the spirit, or whatever term one might use to identify that which is more than the personal ego. It seems to indicate that this person is coming into alignment with his coming transition, and the being's higher aspect is taking over the process. While this is something to be aware of and pay notice to, understand that each death midwife may experience this particular phenomenon in different ways or not at all.

The last story I will share with you is one that happened most recently. Back in 1991, after John, my dearly loved pianist, died, a mutual friend of ours made special airline connections that allowed us to share the flight back from Detroit to West Palm Beach. It was another miracle in that time of miracles because if Michael hadn't been there to catch me when the damn of tears and emotion broke, I do not think the airline attendants would have allowed me to board the plane.

"She'll be all right," he assured them, as he nearly carried me onto the plane. And because he was there, I was. Michael had been a good friend, but after that he had a place in my heart that no one else would ever share.

Michael was a pillar of the gay community, not only in West Palm Beach, but nationwide. He was a tireless gay rights and AIDS activist. He never said no to hosting a benefit at his bar, to volunteering his time, or donating his resources to those in need. He was strong and kind and funny and caring. His heart was bigger than the ocean and it was his loving and generous heart that killed him.

Two years ago, a persistent gnawing feeling in my gut warned that something bad was going to happen to him. I'd since left Florida and, though I loved him and always would, our contact was sporadic. I didn't know what to *do* with that gnawing feeling. Should I call him up and say, "Hi Michael. I'm calling to warn you that something bad is going to happen to you. I don't know where or what or when; it's just a feeling I've got. Have a nice day?" Of course I couldn't do that; but the feeling kept nagging at me.

Just after Easter of 2008 I got an email from another friend living in Florida. In it was a link to a newspaper article and video about Michael being the victim of a murder/suicide. His on-again-off-again lover had turned up the Wednesday before Easter needing money and a place to stay. I never met the man, but Michael's sister had warned him that this man was trouble. Michael told her, "I wouldn't turn a stray dog out onto the street; I won't do it to him."

Apparently the relationship was often explosive, and that night was very bad. Neighbors heard shouting and fighting but didn't call the police. The next evening when Michael didn't arrive at his bar at the usual time, his employees became worried. When someone went to

Michael's apartment to see if he was all right, his lover answered the door and said that Michael was sick.

When Michael failed to show up for work or to call on Good Friday, his employees called the police. They found Michael dead of blunt force trauma to the head and multiple stab wounds. His lover had hung himself in Michael's bedroom.

My worst fears had come true.

At the time of Michael's death, I was fully on the spiritual path of a death midwife. I had witnessed many deaths and had lost so many I loved to disease and accidents that I'd lost count; but I'd never lost a friend to murder.

Once again, I balanced on the precipice. As an empathic person, I saw myself in Michael's apartment, where I'd shared good times with him, now witnessing his murder, seeing the carnage, smelling the blood, feeling what he might have felt as he died…the pain, the shock, the horror, the betrayal. I teetered on the edge of the abyss, ready to fall into utter blackness. *Not this. Not him. Not like this. Why didn't I warn him? How could this happen?*

All my work, all my practice, all my study—nothing soothed the anguish of his brutal murder. I had things to do, workshops to teach, this book to finish, so I needed to be strong and pull it together. *Had I learned nothing?* My psyche insisted that I stop, that I be brought to my knees and humbled once more by soul-scoring grief. It would not let me up until I surrendered to the excruciating pain, until I cooked in it and rode the flame all the way down. Then and only then, did it allow me to rise...as if rising from the ashes of the dead ...with this understanding:

We can walk with death, commune with death, be transformed by death, but we will never conquer death...and being human, we will at times be brought to our knees by death. We can only surrender in deep humility...and be baptized by death into new life again...and again...and again.

That is the lesson Michael taught me.

These are just a few of my experiences with death. The important realization is that each death is unique. Each experience will reflect the individual's life and understanding up to that point. We will learn something new from every one we serve, and we will *never* become experts. Don't ever make the mistake of thinking otherwise. If you do, death will disabuse you of that foolishness, and the lesson will be harsh. Keep an open heart and be grateful for the honor of sharing with another this luminous space of transition, and you will serve both yourself and the dying.

GUIDING BEYOND DEATH

"This life of ours is a sleep and when we die we wake up from the sleep."

– Ali ibn Abi Talib

As the moment of crossing the threshold called death approaches, the soul begins to withdraw upwards from the tips of the toes toward the top of the head. A sensitive death midwife can feel the energy rising, can feel the body growing cooler below as the warmth rises toward the top of the head. If we are present at this crucial moment, we can be of great assistance.

In the ideal situation we would have been able to acquaint those we serve with exercises to facilitate the withdrawal of consciousness. These exercises known as "Lamaze for the dying" were taught by Anna Foos-Graber in her seminal work Deathing. Ideally, they would have practiced these exercises with us and would have become familiar with all of the sensations and phenomena they might encounter as the soul begins to detach from the body.

My suggestion to all wishing to pursue the art of death midwifery is that you read Graber's book and practice the exercises given. Hers was one of the first books I read after John's death and remains one of the best manuals on the concept of deathing. Once you are familiar with how the exercises feel, not only will you be preparing yourself for your own eventual death but then you can also begin coaching those of your patients who are open and willing. Even if they are not familiar with these exercises, there is much we can do.

We can still coach the dying to participate actively in the withdrawal of consciousness from the top of their head or crown chakra. Remind them that they can draw their energy up as if sipping it through a straw and then blowing it out of the top of their head like a whale blowing water from its blow hole or a fountain gushing upwards. If they can tolerate it, we might gently place our hands on the top of the head to guide them. If not, we might hold our hand several inches above the head, finding a place that is not intrusive to that individual we are intending to guide.

We can remind them not to be frightened, that anything they may see or hear or feel is normal. They might feel tingling or buzzing, hear ringing or bells, feel pressure or hot and cold waves, see brilliant white light. This experience can manifest in many ways, all of them normal. As they come closer to detaching from the body, they will very likely feel a great acceleration, and they should not tense against or resist it. Like the laboring mother who, when in the critical stage of transition, has no alternative than to "push!" this acceleration has a life of its own. It is important for the dying to relax and let that velocity sweep them into the arms of God. Everything we can do to remind them that they are safe and that they are not alone will help them to relax, let go, and let God.

We've mentioned the spectrum of death many times. We've spoken about the months, weeks, and days that lead up to crossing the threshold. It is important to remember, however, that the spectrum continues after that threshold is crossed, and the need for our care continues. As mentioned before, in many spiritual traditions, the three days following "death" are considered very important to the soul's journey.

It takes time for the soul to completely detach from the physical body, then from all the subtle bodies. These subtle bodies are known in various traditions by different names such as the etheric, emotional, mental, astral, etheric template, celestial, causal, energy, mental, wisdom, or bliss bodies. It makes no difference what we call them. The important point is that it takes time for each energetic layer to be peeled away, like an onion, from the denser to the finer. We might imagine a rocket ship. As it fires up into the sky, going higher and higher, first one, then another and another of the heavier pieces of the ship fall away until only the capsule is left. That is very much like our soul freeing itself from its earthly vehicle. It takes time.

So what we do to continue our support and guidance for the dying still matters. First we can encourage the family to understand this phenomenon and respect that the deathing process continues for their loved one. Their conduct in the presence of the newly dead is still very important. Maintaining sacred space is important.

The atmosphere should remain reverent, quiet, and respectful of the journey still underway. The focus should still be on the one newly released from the physical body. How sad it is that so many times, the moment "death" occurs, the family disintegrates into chaos, not understanding that their emotions and behavior still affect their loved one. I am sorry to say that I have witnessed fights, verbal and physical, break out in the room with the loved one's body still present. Encourage anyone unable to contain his or her emotions to remove themselves from the sacred space until they can. Even now it is our job to protect the one we serve.

If permissible, place fresh flowers and lit candles around the bed. This feeds the nearly departed spirit's subtle bodies so it will not unintentionally deplete the people gathered around it. Speak to it as "Soul of (name of the departed) to affirm to it that it is no longer in the physical body. (We refer to the departed as "it" since there is no gender in spirit.) Saying prayers, sending love and reminding it that it is safe and good to go into the light are all beneficial.

Allowing children to bear witness to this transition is very beneficial so that from an early age they will know death is a natural part of life and not to be feared. They should not be forced but allowed to touch the body if desired. Letting them share to whatever extent is possible at their stage of development is a gift you can give the next generation so they will become familiar with and more at ease in the presence of death.

In any case, encourage the family to allow the body to rest undisturbed for as long as possible before moving it from sacred space. Again, this gives the spirit time to continue its work of fully disengaging.

My own preference when I die is to leave my body undisturbed for the full three days. This would allow time for rituals and vigiling with the remaining time spent in refrigeration until cremation. That may not be the choice for many, especially those who choose to be organ donors, but it is my choice. My loved ones know it and will respect it when the time comes. Without question, we always respect and follow the final wishes of the dead, which hopefully are known to the family.

In some parts of the world home funerals are allowed, and this can be a wonderful choice for some. In the resources section at the back of the book there is a list of web sites of organizations that can help with that option.

For some, having an overnight vigil with the body is a profoundly moving experience. This might include bathing and grooming the body, singing and performing specialized rituals to honor the newly departed spirit. Then simply sitting with the body as night falls, lighting candles, perhaps playing music that is meaningful and evocative, and simply communing, praying, and witnessing as the moon dies and the sun is reborn.

Especially during those three days after crossing the threshold, our continued guidance and reassurance is beneficial to the newly dead. We can continue to support and guide as we did before, doing our process work in preparation to the practice. Only now we touch and commune exclusively with spirit.

A few words of caution are offered. First, as mentioned before, it is best to open and close each session of the practice. Keeping the lines of communication open can be very draining. Second, be very sure that it is truly support and not distraction that you offer. The newly dead have much to do so we do not want to annoy them with idle chitchat. We are there simply to support and guide, to remind them that they are safe in their new surroundings, that they are not alone, and, should they encounter the light, it is good to embrace it. This is a wonderful time to pray for their continued journey into new life.

When they are ready, and if we are open and aware, the dead can and will often choose to communicate with us. This can happen in many ways, and we will discuss a few, though a thorough discourse on after-death communications is beyond the scope of this book. Suggested reading on the topic is listed in the resource pages at the back.

The easiest and least startling way for the dead to communicate is through dream-like episodes. How these visitations might be perceived is highly individual, but their quality is quite different from normal dreams. You need to discover how this works for you. I know it is a visit when the dead come to me in a "white space." There is usually nothing but white surrounding them, and they generally will look very luminous. There is no plot line to the "dream," but only communion, often of a very deep and sometimes prophetic nature.

After John died, I began my study of thanatology in earnest. Part of that study was taking a college course on death and dying. As part of the course requirements we had to make a presentation. I decided to host a presentation on AIDS awareness, inviting local heads of AIDS organizations to speak. A friend of John's and mine was Mary Fisher, an artist turned AIDS activist when her husband died of the disease and she found herself to be HIV positive. She was an assistant to President Gerald Ford and, at the 1992 republican convention, made a passionate speech about the need for AIDS awareness. She agreed to be a speaker at my presentation.

I needed a space for this presentation and didn't know the campus facilities at all. One night as I slept, I found myself in the back of a small auditorium I'd never seen before, sitting in a row of seats next to John. Heads together, we looked over the space, and he asked me if it would suit my purpose. I told him it would be a perfect space for the presentation. The next day, my professor brought me to an auditorium. It was the exact one from my "dream" with John.

Dreams are one of the most common ways for the dead to communicate, but there are countless others. Scents related to the deceased may appear unexpectedly. In the hospital right after John died, I washed my hands at the sink in his room. The smell of the liquid soap was very distinct. It was a smell I'd never encountered before, and I related it strictly to that experience with John.

Shortly after he died and for two years thereafter, the smell of that soap would greet me in the strangest of places. At home, in the car, at a restaurant, in hotels; even when I moved from Florida to Arizona, that smell followed me. I came to understand it was John's way of saying hi, of letting me know he was around, checking in on me, seeing if I was okay. For two years that smell would appear on and off, anywhere and everywhere; then it happened less and less frequently and finally faded altogether. It is my belief that the dying will check in with us for a while. Then their work takes them further and further from the consciousness of those still in the body until their vibration becomes too fine or too high for us to perceive at all.

Messages can come from unlikely sources. On my thirty-fifth birthday—the last one John celebrated with me—he told me, "You'll never be more beautiful than you are right now." It was a lovely thing to say, though at the time I thought to myself, "What? Does that mean it's downhill all the way from here?" Then about two weeks after John's death I met some friends at one of our old haunts. I walked up to the bar and a person I barely knew turned around, looked at me, and said, "You'll never be more beautiful than you are right now." For someone on the fringes of my life to say the same thing John had said on one of our last days together, word for word, out of nowhere, completely stunned me. I knew without question, that it was not a coincidence, but another example of the many ways the dead can communicate with us.

In order to hear the dying, we must be aware of seeming coincidences and synchronicities. Messages may come through dreams or rainbows or animals. Books can drop off the shelf to an open page that has a powerful message just for you. Refrains from a special song might come over the radio at just the right moment. You might feel soft caresses on the back of your neck in an empty room. There are so many ways the dead can reach us—if we allow ourselves to be open to them.

Assisting Those Left Behind

Very likely, if you are reading these pages you have been initiated onto this path of death midwifery by bearing the loss of a loved one. You've felt the lash of loss tear your soul to shreds, and you have healed or perhaps been transformed by your grief. Even if this is familiar terrain for you, I ask you to walk it again with me as we look through the eyes of others who are left behind.

There is no pain greater than the loss of a loved one, and no two losses are ever the same. Grieving the deaths of our beloveds, be they spouses, parents, children, siblings, friends or pets, is the hardest work any of us will ever do. Though our focus as death midwives is on the dying, once the threshold is crossed and the initial three days is past, we can offer support and guidance to those left behind.

Everyone grieves differently; but in order to heal, one must accept that grief work is not optional. One who tries to escape or deny grief will ultimately pay a huge price, physically, mentally, emotionally, energetically, and/or spiritually. "Try" is the operative word here for no one can truly escape the arduous work of grief. Whether one chooses to face grief consciously with awareness or to be blindsided by it and suffer its rampages by default will determine if the experience will ultimately be healing (and potentially even transformative) or if it will cripple one's soul for life.

Loss, grief, and mourning are dark fathomless terrains littered with jagged shards of memories, broken dreams, unfinished business, and regret. It is the end of a relationship ***in its present form.*** Shock, horror, suffering, denial, anger, rage, depression, despair, and longing are some of its earlier landscapes. There is no way to bypass them; there is no detour. The only way to travel this bleak terrain is to bravely walk through it. We who walk the earth must make our way through this darkness. It is our cross to bear in this material world. No one can carry it for us; but we can act as voices in the wilderness calling out to our brothers and sisters struggling in the dark, reaching out our hands to show them that we are there and that where the darkness ends, the light once again returns.

Grief is the price we pay for loving, and, for most of us, it is a price well paid. The pain of grieving will be equal to the joy of loving. There is no escaping that as there is always balance. We could try to avoid the pain of parting by deadening out hearts to love but at what price? The question we must ask ourselves is, "Will I accept the dear price for loving? If you are still reading these pages, the answer, we hope, is..."Yes!"

Having been bloodied by grief, the agony of our own losses can bathe the wounds of those now left behind with the balm of compassion. Compassion is the ability to remember. We express it by listening—to their stories, to their fears, to their longings and regrets, and sometimes to their anger. Those who have not yet walked through the bleak wilderness of grief may turn and run, but we will stay…and we will listen. What those left behind need the most is to be heard and assured that all the conflicting emotions and physical symptoms they might be experiencing – the insomnia or overwhelming need for sleep; the inability to read; the loss of appetite or loss of memory—are normal in the dark landscape of grief…and that they can survive it. Our assurance is vital, for in the beginning it may seem that this grief will surely kill them.

Again, as death midwives the goal is to *be* more than to *do.* Just as we were present with the dying, we strive to *be* present with the staggering pain of those left behind. Without judgment we now keep open sacred space for that loved one to cry, rant and rave, laugh, reminisce or whatever else is needed to begin the long road to healing. We do not spout platitudes. We do not hide behind clichés. We do not tell the grieving how to feel or what to think. Do not underestimate for a second the value of that gift for few can offer it. Most want to fix it or to escape. Others unwittingly shut the grieving process down with thoughtless words. Many people simply cannot be present to the unpredictable force of nature that is grief but we can. That is the gift we offer to those left behind.

Beyond that, are there things we can *do?* We can offer suggestions on many things. If there is an interest, we can provide grieving families with resources for home or green funerals. When the time is right, we can offer books on grief and provide information on support groups, some of which specialize. There are groups for parents who have lost young children; for those whose loved one was murdered or committed suicide; for children who have been traumatized by loss, etc. If desired, we can recommend private counseling services. As death midwives, we want to know what resources our communities offer. The resources section at the back of this book will offer some suggestions, as well.

Keep in mind that we are not grief counselors, and it is not our job to companion those left behind on their journey through the dark terrain of grief indefinitely. Our job is to be there at the beginning when it is darkest, to be fully present to their suffering and willing to share their burden for a time so they may regain their bearings. We then act as liaisons, helping them find the resources and support needed to begin the arduous journey they ultimately must make alone.

A Word about Self Care

We act as conduits for divine light and love, creating and maintaining sacred space for long periods of time and for many people. This skill involves both art and technique that require great personal resources. It is extremely important that we, whose focus is so attentively on others, learn to care for ourselves as well.

All caretakers must guard against burnout, and we are no exception. We must take time to do the things that will rebalance, refresh, renew, recharge, and restore us. In order to quench the thirst of others, the well must be continually replenished.

At the end of a day as a death midwife, it is important to have a self-care ritual in place. As part of the ritual, take off and clean the special set of clothes consecrated to the service of death midwifery. After that initial step of cleansing, the ritual can be anything that sooths, balances, and restores. It could be a walk in nature, playing with a beloved pet, listening to soothing music, or my personal favorite, soaking in a steaming tub of water laced with relaxing essential oils. Be sure to drink a lot of water and have a healthy meal. Keeping a journal of what was witnessed in that sacred space is very beneficial. After spending so much time in the space between worlds, make sure to actively re-engage in the world of the living—and be sure to get a good night's sleep.

Continuing self-care comes in many forms. First, it must be understood that we cannot be all things to all people. There will be some instances where what we offer is not a good fit for the one we wished to serve. We must accept this with grace. At times it may not be a good fit for us, and we must be able to accept that with grace too. The art of death midwifery should only be undertaken when it works for everyone involved. It is always a gift, and gifts can sometimes be returned.

Do not take on more patients than you can reasonably serve. It is better to spend more quality time with one person than bits of time with many. In this culture of the ten-minute attention span, sustained presence is becoming a rare commodity. The miracles come with time spent, so do not fall into the trap of spreading yourself too thin.

We should have a daily spiritual practice that sustains us. The process outlined in this book can be used if you do not already have something in place. Ultimately, you need something that feeds the soul. Whether that is communing with nature, journaling, chanting, praying, or meditating is up to you but it should be done daily, even if only for 20 minutes.

Other ways we can strengthen our vessel is by taking care with what we eat and drink, what we read and watch on television, and by getting enough sleep each night. All these things will strengthen our vessel and enhance our ability to be clear, strong conduits.

After each death midwifery session, take time to restore balance before seeing another person. At the end of each day of service, take time to fully divest yourself of any emotions or conditions that do not belong to you.

Journaling is an important tool for discovery and renewal. I cannot recommend it strongly enough. Although the journal can be written in the traditional way, it does not need to be. Speaking words into a recorder or expressing your thoughts and feelings through art, poetry, or making collages can work just as well. Let your imagination dictate the medium, and let it flow! In time, your journaling can become a valuable and validating resource.

In our modern culture sleep tends to be underrated. It is as if the need to sleep eight or more hours a night is a sign of weakness or laziness. It is no wonder that we see so much discontent and rage in our society. Many of us are sleep deprived! Not only does much healing and rebalancing occur during sleep, but sleep is the natural entranceway to our experience of death. It is our way of practicing crossing the border from the physical to the non-physical. Perhaps that is why so many in our culture have difficulty sleeping or deprive themselves of enough of it. Perhaps an unconscious fear of death drives us from restful, restorative sleep, as if we will never awaken…as if death is the end rather than just a change of forms. Giving yourself the gift of a full night of deep and peaceful sleep is an extreme act of self love.

Finally, seek like-minded spirits and support. Though nearly all will benefit from the art of death midwifery in some form, and many will grow from the inner work required, few will be called to walk this path of service in depth. It is, therefore, very important for those who are called, to build a community of like-minded souls so we can share our experiences, thoughts, concerns, and joys. With that in mind, we have created an Internet Google group for those interested in the art of death midwifery. It is a restricted group, but the only requirement to be invited is that you have a sincere interest in this topic. In the resources section at the back of this book is listed the web site address to request an invitation to join our budding community.

Death Midwifery as a Way of Life or as a Living?

Often the question is asked about the art of death midwifery as a career, as a way of making a living. I'd like to share some thoughts on what it is, what it is not, and what it might become.

From a personal viewpoint, my practice of the art of death midwifery has been offered as a gift. Though at times, I was paid as a hospice companion or home health aide, the practice of this specific art has been freely given to any who accept the gift. Usually this has been through volunteering at hospitals, hospices, or nursing homes. That is my choice. That is what I am comfortable with, what spirit guides me to do, and I am blessed to be able to practice in this way.

Primarily, this is a path of service; but I can see a time when there will be those who devote themselves to it exclusively and make a living doing it. We live in a material world, after all, and this valuable art is time intensive.

We are on the leading edge of a massive change of consciousness in this culture. So many of the ways we have done things up to this point are being re-evaluated. As the baby boomers reach retirement, death and how we wish to approach our final moments will be looked at with new eyes. It is already beginning to happen. This art has been slowly simmering over many years, waiting for the right time to be re-introduced to the world. That time is now.

There will be some of you who will pioneer this art as a career. As pioneers, you will undoubtedly encounter challenges, misunderstandings, and perhaps even opposition. How to find those who want your services, how to charge for them, and where death midwifery fits into the continuum of care are all questions that will need addressing. Those of you on the leading edge will need clarity, integrity, tenacity, and training.

Some essentials:

We must have **clarity** that, when we practice the art of death midwifery, we are not healers. We are guides. We are conduits. We offer energetic support—but we are **not** healers. We are not medical death midwives, but spiritual and energetic ones. Be very clear on this point, with yourself and with others so that there is no misunderstanding.

Integrity is the cornerstone of all that we offer. It should be expressed in our conduct, in our purpose, in our demeanor, in our inner work, in our dealings with those we serve and with whom we come in contact in the normal course of our lives. We must be meticulous in our attitudes and behavior, as the totality of who we are either strengthens or weakens our vessel, our ability to be strong and pure conduits.

It takes **tenacity** to do the arduous inner work required to continue the practice even through times of doubt and despair. Make no mistake—you will face those times. It also takes tenacity to face challenge and perhaps even ridicule from those who might misunderstand what we offer. Remember, though, we are never alone in this work. At all times our angelic friends and assistants are there to lean on when we feel weak.

Training is essential. Every organization that uses volunteers to support the dying requires them to go through some sort of training program. If you wish to practice the art of death midwifery, you will need that specialized training as well.

This book is a beginning. In the resources section at the back are listed other books and DVDs that are highly recommended for those sincerely interested in this path of service.

In addition, we've created an educational organization, Create Sacred Space for Conscious Transitions, dedicated to the art of death midwifery. It is open to assist those interested in this path. We are currently restructuring our studies to offer some of the teachings either online or using various other advances in technology in the hope of making this art available to more people more readily. To deepen the practice, we may offer occasional weekend intensives in Virginia Beach, Va. The introductory courses are suited to nearly anyone who is interested in approaching death, their own or that of others, with more consciousness. Each successive level of study builds upon the preceding one; each has its own suggested reading and writing assignments. These offerings, while certainly focused upon serving others, in fact, have the most profound and potentially transformative effect upon those who take them. We are discovering that even if the only person that is ever served by this study is oneself, a tremendous shift occurs in this world that should never be taken lightly!

Our hope is to inspire a core of trained death midwives who will make themselves available to families to practice the art of death midwifery for their dying loved ones, whether they are at home, in hospice, in a nursing home, or in the hospital.

These are just some of the considerations in choosing how we wish to practice this art, which is being born again into this modern culture and which will need nurturing. We reach out to each of you who feel the call to his path of service, who wish to join the ranks of death midwives. Together we can change the way we view death and treat the dying. We can remember, for ourselves and for others, that we are safe...we are surrounded by love...and we are *never* alone.

QUESTIONS AND ANSWERS

We've been asked some fascinating and valuable questions by students in our workshops. In this section, we'll include some that we think may be on the minds of others as well.

I do Reiki healing. Should I ground myself? How about my patient?

Reiki is a valuable tool to offer as a part of the art of death midwifery, but with modifications. Each individual will need to experiment to find what works best. My suggestion, however, would be to ground yourself *after* finishing your time with the one dying. Up until then, you are traveling through many levels of consciousness, some very low and some quite high. My intuition tells me that grounding ahead of time will work against the ability to do that easily. Keeping your feet solidly on the ground while focusing and directing divine light and love will provide all the grounding you need during your time with the dying.

As for the ones dying...**DO NOT EVER** ground them. They need to withdraw their consciousness upwards toward the crown chakra so grounding their energy would hamper them. Remember always to do no harm!

How can I prepare for my own death?

Buy a copy of Anya-Foos Graber's book Deathing. She has a series of exercises drawn from the wisdom of the Tibetan Book of the Dead. These exercises, a kind of Lamaze for the dying, will help you become familiar with the sensations and phenomena we encounter during our deathing process. If these exercises are learned and practiced, then at the time of our actual death, we will be able to consciously participate in it with awareness and without fear, rather than by default and in chaos.

I've never been with anyone as they died, but it sounds like something I'd like to do. Do I really need all this training and preparation?

Yes, you do, for many reasons. First, because it is incredibly disrespectful to those we serve not to be as informed and educated about what they are going through as possible. They generally have enough people around them who are clueless; they do not need another ill-equipped well-wisher in their presence.

Second, depending on the situation, you may encounter some very challenging situations, smells, sights, sounds, etc., that you will need to be prepared for. You need to be comfortable in any situation that might arise. You cannot create sacred space if you are shocked or upset by your surroundings.

We can make the mistake of romanticizing death and our roles as death midwives; but just like birth, death can be and often is a messy affair. Especially in hospitals and nursing homes, we can be bombarded by so many stimuli that it can be overwhelming. By being intellectually prepared and by gradually working our way up to more challenging environments, we serve both our patients *and* ourselves. It is important that we know and respect our personal boundaries and not exceed them even with the best of intentions. Not all of us will be comfortable in the I.C.U., and that is okay. Not all of us will be comfortable in nursing homes, and that is okay. Not all of us will thrive in home environments, and that is okay. To put our service to the best possible use, we need to be honest about our strengths and weaknesses. That requires experience and a continued willingness to learn.

In "the process," how will I know when the levels of consciousness open up? What will it look like or feel like?

When we talk about the inner work we do in preparing to practice the art of death midwifery, we are dealing with highly subjective things. Each person's inner world is a unique landscape; each of us senses and experiences things differently. I cannot tell you definitively how *you* will perceive this expanding of consciousness potentially from the lowest epsilon levels to the highest lambda levels. What I can do is share with you what it is like *for me* at my present level of awareness and experience.

My inner work is intuited primarily and most strongly by *feeling.* I am acutely aware of sensations. Perhaps this has a lot to do with my early training as a dancer.

Dancers are taught not to rely on mirrors to know what a position looked like, but to go inside and know what it *feels* like. I feel things very strongly; therefore, for me, I know that I'm reaching that place in my inner warm-up when the levels of consciousness are expanding by *feeling* a counter-resistant stretching through the center of my body...like a thick band of saltwater taffy being stretched thin...or a thick rubber band being pulled at each end. That is my signal.

Someone who senses energy with inner vision or inner hearing would very likely experience this entirely differently, so it is incumbent on each individual practitioner to become very familiar with how he or she experiences the interior world. No one can tell you how that will be for you. Only dedication to this inner work will inform you. I can say with certainty that if you do this work faithfully, you *will* learn how this manifests for *you*. You will *know*. This is where trust and faith come in, and a death midwife must draw on these two strengths often.

What do I tell people I do? How do I explain this to them?

This is a very good question and not as simple as it seems. Truly, it depends on the specific situation.

We may tell people that we support the dying in a profound way by creating and maintaining sacred space so that whatever needs to take place can take place with reverence, dignity, and grace.

We may tell them that we act as energetic and spiritual guides who provide support.

We may tell them that, like birth midwives, we support and companion those we serve in their birth into a new life.

Or we may simply say that we bring company and soothing music to those who might otherwise be "alone."

Depending on who I am talking to, their situation and their level of awareness, I have said all of these things. It is important to "learn the language" of those you serve and speak to them in it. Speaking French to an Italian will only confuse and frustrate. How we speak to someone who is agnostic will be different than how we might speak to a fundamentalist Christian or to a metaphysician. Being able to communicate in many "languages" is part of the skill of a death midwife.

What I have never said is that I am a conduit for God's love and light. That is, in its purest sense, what I aspire to be, but I never make that claim. For while it is true that we seek permission from those we serve, at the same time, we must offer the great work in secret…in deep humbleness, that we may be used to that purpose for no other reason but that *we can do no less.*

Discretion and sensitivity must be used when speaking of what we offer. Know to whom you are speaking – family, hospital administration, or a person who is actively dying – and tailor the information to that specific audience in a language they understand.

How do I approach a hospital about offering my services?

Whether for a hospital, hospice, or nursing home, the best and easiest way is to volunteer your services. First contact the volunteer coordinator. Each facility will have their own procedure and training that must be completed, and many require certain medical tests and inoculations. In the case of a hospital or nursing home, let them know you are specifically offering your services to those who are dying. That way they can focus your volunteer work to the appropriate department. Some hospitals have designated palliative care or hospice units.

If you wish to be paid for your services then the best approach at this time might be as a consultant. In this case you would write up a proposal stating the length of the contract, the hourly rate, what services you would provide, and the result your services would bring. This would be submitted to the head of the appropriate department for consideration. In time, it is my hope that death midwives will be considered an essential part of the care team and would find positions as paid staff; but, presently, we are in the pioneer stages, so it will be up to those on the leading edge to bring that to fruition.

Another possibility is for educated death midwives to be retained by the family to act as support in a variety of situations – home, hospital, hospice or nursing facility. In this way, the death midwife can more easily circumnavigate the sometimes difficult waters of various bureaucracies. This work could either be supported by love donations or by a fee arranged with the family.

How can I serve someone who has done a terrible thing, a murderer for example? Isn't there a hell? Does everyone go "into the light?"

If you are asking this question, the answer is most likely you cannot. We, as death midwives, do not judge or condemn. That is not our job. It is not our place. We do not have that right. We are not the arbiters of another's soul.

Whether there is a hell is not our concern. Our patient's ultimate destination is not our concern. **We treat each one we serve with the same unconditional love and acceptance or we do not enter the room.** This rule is inviolate.

Now, that being said, we are all human beings. We all have our strengths and weaknesses. If we find ourselves in a situation where we cannot be in that place of unconditional love and acceptance, the best course is **not to serve.** We do not have to serve everyone. It is perfectly fine to know our limitations and to honor them. It is **not** okay to bring our judgment and condemnation into the sacred space of the dying!

If we do our job, if we create and maintain this sacred space, if we are strong and pure conduits for divine light and love, miraculous transformations, that we may never know the full extent of, can and do happen; but that is between the one dying and her conception of God. We, as death midwives, respect the privacy and sanctity of that relationship.

From my rebirthing experience, I learned that I was born kicking and screaming into this life. If we die the way we live, how can I make sure I do not go out kicking and screaming as well?

Go deeply into this work, and you will come to know that death is not an enemy. It is not something to fight against. When the time is right, it is something to embrace like a lover. The more consciousness we can bring into this transition, the more we will see it for what it truly is: a birth into new life. We had to die to where we came from in order to be born into this life. We must die to this one to be born into the next. It is not something to fear, but we tend to fear what we do not understand. Use your time wisely upon this earth to sit down with death, have a cup of tea, and become friends.

Have you ever experienced someone on the other side of the threshold of death taking over your body to communicate with loved ones left behind?

No, I haven't. While I have had communication from the other side of the threshold, the dead have never tried to use my body to communicate with others. There are those, though, with the sensitivity to be trance mediums. My suggestion, however, is to make it clear to the dead that they should not enter your body. I would set clear boundaries concerning that. Make it clear to them that you can hear them, and it is okay to communicate with you, but they are to stay outside of your body. You can relay their messages perfectly well in that way.

What happens if you visit and they don't die?

That happens all the time. No one can tell with exactitude when another will die. We have clues. We can make educated guesses, but no one can predict the time of another's death. So often, for whatever reason, we may need to leave before the actual time of death. We may be returning, we may not, but in any case, we always place our patient directly into the hands of the angels, who will continue the work we began together.

What if the family objects? What if their faith representative (i.e., priest, pastor, reverend, etc.) objects? What if the facility staff is less than cooperative?

If the one dying is able to voice his wishes, then we would ask that he make his request for our services known to his family, pastor, and medical staff. If he is unable to make his wishes clear, it is important not to take an adversarial role. As mentioned before, in hospital and nursing home environments, my preference is to work in solitude. Should a family member or clergy member come in and seem uncomfortable with my presence, I would leave and come back at another time.

With staff, for the most part, I find that even if they do not understand what I am doing, they appreciate the gentle and loving time spent with their patient. Often the space created envelops them as well. They feel more relaxed and balanced, and they really appreciate that! However, sometimes, they need to do complicated procedures that require a good deal of time. In that case, again, I would excuse myself and return at a better time.

This is never a contest or a battle. We are like water that flows around the rocks. Sometimes we have to realize that the situation is just not conducive to creating sacred space. In that case, we move on and put our attention where it would best serve.

How do others know you're not a quack?

Oh, I let comments like those just roll off my back. Bah-doom chink! Seriously, they will know by the manner in which you present yourself—by your words, your demeanor and your essence. You must present yourself with integrity, express yourself clearly, and invoke a sense of peace, sincerity, and commitment.

In the beginning, there may be those who, despite your best efforts, will consider you a quack. Again, this is something newly brought back to this culture, and those on the forefront must be strong enough to weather the skepticism that greets new ideas.

Devote your efforts to growing in your practice. Study, study, study! If you do the inner work required, even those who may not fully understand will feel the energy field that will surround you.

What are your credentials? And how did you get credentialed?

I am an ordained interfaith minister with a Doctorate of Divinity in Death as a Transition and After Death Communications. I earned these credentials through years of study and practice in the field of death and dying.

The most important credential I have is the time I have spent in the presence of the dying since 1991. They are my teachers. They are the ones to whom I bow. All the reading and writing in the world will not make up for actually serving the dying. All the credentials in the world will not equal deeply experiencing and fully mourning the loss of those you love. Those losses, those experiences, are my true credentials, as your losses and experiences will be yours.

In the art of death midwifery, as in all arts, training is essential. To address that need, I have created an educational organization. Create Sacred Space for Conscious Transitions will offer study in this art through various mediums.

Can you hurt the person?

The art of death midwifery cannot physically hurt a person. In our inexperience, we can, however, do things that can energetically complicate the deathing process or simply annoy or offend the dying. These things have been mentioned in other parts of this book so I will not reiterate them here.

Is this like "assisted" suicide?

That is an excellent question and one you will no doubt encounter in your practice as a death midwife. The answer is unequivocally no. This is in no way like assisted suicide. To be very clear, we in the art of death midwifery do not offer any kind of physical care. We serve as spiritual and energetic guides only. We do not touch machines or give medications. We do nothing to hasten anyone's death. We bear witness to this sacred event, supporting the dying with unconditional love and acceptance. Acting as conduits for divine light, we do not know in what form perfect healing will manifest for the one we serve, but we know that it *will* manifest in divine right timing in divine right order.

How do you stay optimistic?

I think it goes beyond staying optimistic. I think it is about strengthening our vessels, enough to withstand both the joy and the sorrow we will encounter. It is not one or the other but both. That is the nature of life. So, too, is it the nature of death. To deny one only weakens the other, so we must be strong enough to hold the tension between the opposites. That is where the juice is.

As a death midwife, I am granted the incredible gift of being in the presence of those making the most mysterious and awesome of transitions. I am allowed to witness a bit of this time of transformation. Yes, it is an ending of the life we know for a life yet to be discovered. Yes, there is sadness at that ending. There can be fear of pain and suffering and fear of the unknown; but there can also be joy for the ones beginning this new adventure, joy at leaving the confines of the flesh for the freedom of pure spirit, and joy at losing the illusion of separation and regaining the knowledge that we are one with God.

This joy does not come automatically, but only through years of communing with the dying. Mixed with that joy are tears; but we learn to contain both the tears and the joy simultaneously…and that is a gift beyond gold.

Birthing Ourselves Through Death

Nothing you can lose by dying is half as precious as the readiness to die, which is man's charter of nobility.

– George Santayana

If we look deeply, we come to this path of service so that we ourselves can be healed of the fear of death. If we are honest, we understand that we give the gift we would most like to receive. We've likely found ourselves on this path because of a horrific loss or a life-changing event. We are here because we *have* to be; but no matter how much we'd like to think we offer this gift altruistically, in truth, we are ultimately serving ourselves as much as, if not more than, any other human being.

There is nothing wrong in this. In fact, the more we practice this art, the more we are in the presence of the dying, the more we prepare for our own eventual death. The more we prepare for our own transition, the more likely we will be able to embrace this inevitable change of forms with greater consciousness and grace. If the only person we ever serve as death midwife turns out to be ourselves, that alone would cause a major shift in cosmic consciousness and be a blessing to all

As mentioned before, in Anya Foos-Graber's ground-breaking work, Deathing, she offers a series of exercises based on the Tibetan Book of the Dead that facilitate the withdrawal of consciousness from the crown chakra. It is highly recommended that you purchase this book and learn the exercises, either alone or with a partner. That will greatly assist you at the time of your death. If you are alone, you may record your voice as you read the exercises aloud. Do this for yourself!

Birthing mothers have learned the value of preparing mentally and physically for the challenge they face. It is time to understand the value of preparing for our death so that we need not be caught off guard or filled with anguish. Preparing for our death goes beyond writing wills, establishing medical power of attorney and making funeral arrangements, it means preparing for the actual process of death. Instead of death happening randomly, we can, in many cases, participate actively in this amazing transformation. Even in the case of "accidental" death, if we have prepared, we may understand what is happening and not be frozen with shock.

If we have the courage to delve into the root of all fear, to dig into the dark recesses of our souls...would not the fear of death most likely be the most primal? How much of our lives are predicated on the fear of death? How much are we controlled and manipulated by our fear of this transition? If we could sit with death, be familiar with it in its many forms and faces...if we could become friends with death...sitting with it and sharing a cup of tea...how might the way we live our lives change?

THE END? NOT SO FINAL THOUGHTS

Death - the last sleep? No the final awakening.

– Walter Scott

Just as death is not the end, but rather a new beginning, so we have come to the end of this book, which is also not the end, but instead, another beginning. After reading this book, it is our hope that you, dear reader, will feel the urge to go further down this path of the art of death midwifery. We hope that you will feel the pull to explore more deeply this magnificent and awe-inspiring transition we call death, to develop a relationship with death that need not be adversarial, to be open to the possibility that death can be both a teacher and a friend.

This guide you hold in your hands is just the beginning. To help support you in your new relationship with death, a resource page is located at the end of this book. On it are web sites and suggested reading to continue your study and supply you with some of the tools you will need to become a death midwife. That, too, is only a start.

In addition to this book, it is our intention to create CDs and DVDs to enhance, inform, and deepen your understanding and practice of the art of death midwifery. That is the next step in our mission of training the death midwives who will be needed in the coming years. As this renaissance with death and life unfolds, you will be needed. Look around and you will see how so many cultural norms are dying only to be reborn in new and better-fitting forms. It is the nature of life and so, too, is it the nature of death.

Remember, we are on the leading edge of a major shift of consciousness concerning death and how we want that powerful and important transition to take place. We have the power to reshape the current culture with its fear and denial of death. Together, we can help the world remember that life continues beyond death, that consciousness continues indefinitely, eternally, ever evolving, and ever expanding beyond our capability to comprehend.

Remember, too, that just as each life matters, each death also matters. Everything matters. *Everything matters.* If we support even one person in having a more sacred, dignified, and reverent death, we make a huge contribution to this shift of consciousness. If the only person we ever midwife through this mystifying transition is ourselves, we've done something powerful for the planet. We've performed a major act of alchemy, changing fear into awe, suffering into transformation. We've been conduits for sacred magic. That is no small act.

These may be new ideas in this 21st century western culture, but the time is right to bring this understanding back down to the earth. It's time to allow death to take its rightful place on the canvas of life. If we take the time to look deeply into its mystery, we may not know it fully, but we can become far more familiar, far more comfortable and far more at ease with its inevitability. We can transform death from a tragedy into an art. Dare to be an artist!

When I Die
Joseph R. Lee

Do not seek me at my grave for my body has been taken by the earth and the roots of strong trees have drawn my soul into the air

Seek me in the softness of the new green as I uncurl with the spring ferns

Seek me in the summer leaves when my voice is hidden in the rustling of that maple in the far corner of the yard

Seek me in the ashes of an evening fire, after all our friends have left, when they are stirred in the morning, I am resting in the faint warm embers

Seek me in the sigh of my lover on a long fall night and speed there and cradle his hand and find me alive again as I play across the face I have kissed which remembers my scent

And when my lover is gone, and when my home bears another's name, and when my words are turned brown and dark and indistinguishable and feed a new garden, I will be free to remember only the Light from which I flowed and remembering my Home I will laugh at my self and wonder how I ever forgot.

Life into Life – Epilogue

It is the summer of 2008. It's been seventeen years since the death of my darling dog, Maggie Mae. No puppy overlap for me; the thought of having another dog was far too painful. Seventeen years of healing in the presence of the dying; years and years of inner work. Shifts happened, synchronicities congealed…and a miracle manifested. His name is Bodhi.

Bodhi, Sanskrit for "enlightenment," materialized rather suddenly (or was it?) this June. The exact, rather rare breed (Havanese) I'd daydreamed about manifested at a wonderful price from a breeder not five miles from our home. I wasn't even looking for him. His brother from a different litter came bouncing down our street one day. We stopped to ask his owners what he was and where he came from. We got a name and phone number and within the week, Bodhi was ours. A little white dog…come to bring light and new life.

A place in my heart that was sealed tight by Maggie's death is now thrown open. I didn't even realize it was closed. This newly opened place in my heart feels so vulnerable, so tender, so raw. It is both scary and exhilarating to love and be loved so unconditionally. The responsibility for this little life's care is at the same time sobering and empowering.

I look at this little white dog, so filled with love, and already the shadow of knowing one day he will die pricks my heart. But I have a chance. I have a chance to do for Bodhi what I was not able to do for Maggie. I will love him enough to watch him die…and that will be a gift for both of us.

A CALL TO THE WORLD COMMUNITY

If after reading this book you feel called in any way to support this work, we welcome you. Not everyone will feel the pull to become a death midwife, but many will embrace the importance of this service. We are birthing this movement for a more conscious sacred transition, and each of you can play midwife to it.

We welcome your input, your thoughts, talents, abilities, and resources. We need help bringing this work into being. Your support is vital, for we are all in this together, and together we will offer a more loving, peaceful, sacred birth into new life to those who seek it.

This work is growing…one heart at a time. If you feel it in your heart to help, please contact us:

Create Sacred Space for Conscious Transitions
P.O. Box 10543
Virginia Beach, VA. 23450

Email – info@deathmidwifery.com

Web site – www.deathmidwifery.com

Thank you. Thank you. Thank you!

Reading and Resource List

Books on Meditation

Meditation for Beginners – Jack Kornfield
Meditation for Dummies – Stephan Bodian

Books on Breathwork

Science of Breath – Ramacharaka Yogi
The Yoga of Breath – Richard Rosen
Conscious Breathing – Gay Hendricks, Ph.D.
Dance of Breath – Kathleen Barratt

Books on Angel Communication

A Book of Angels – Sophy Burnham
Ask Your Angels – Alma Daniel, Timothy Wyllie & Andrew Ramer
Angels 101 – Doreen Virtue, Ph.D.

Books on Vocalizing

Toning – Laurel Elizabeth
Set Your Voice Free – Roger Love
Healing Sounds: The Power of Harmonics - Jonathan Goldman

Books on Science and Intention

Entangled Minds – Dean Radin
The Intention Experiment – Lynne McTaggart
The Field Updated Ed: The Quest for the Secret Force of the Universe - Lynne McTaggart
The Origin of Consciousness in the Breakdown of the Bicameral Mind – Julian Jaynes, Ph.D.

Books on Death

Deathing – Anya Foos-Graber
The Tibetan Book of Living and Dying – Sogyal Rinpoche
Final Gifts – Maggie Callanan & Patricia Kelley
Sacred Dying – Megory Anderson
The Tibetan Book of the Dead – translated by W.Y. Evans-Wentz
Gifts for the Living – BettyClare Moffatt, M.A.
Who Dies? – Stephen Levine
Home with God – Neale Donald Walsch
Graceful Exits – Sushila Blackman
The Sacred Art of Dying – Kenneth Kramer

Books on the Survival of Consciousness after Death

What Survives? – edited by Gary Doore, Ph.D.
No Death – Hugh Lynn Cayce & Edgar Cayce
The Place We Call Home – Robert J. Grant
Dion Fortune's Book of the Dead – Dion Fortune

Life after Death: The Burden of Proof by Deepak Chopra
Practicing Conscious Living and Dying – Annamaria Hemingway

Books on Grieving

How to Go on Living When Someone You Love Dies – Therese A. Rando
The Grief Recovery Handbook – John W. James & Frank Cherry
Companions through the Darkness – Stephanie Ericsson
Understanding Your Grief - Alan D. Wolfelt
Healing Grief – James Van Praagh

Books on After Death Communication

Hello from Heaven – Bill & Judy Guggenheim
Love Beyond Life – Joel Martin & Patricia Romanowski
We Don't Die – George Anderson
Talking To Heaven – James Van Praagh
One Last Time – John Edward

DVD

As You Die – P.M.H. Atwater

CDs

Life Beyond Words – Jennifer Taylor
Music for the Dying – Donalyn Gross

Listening at the Threshold – Threshold Choir
Tenderly Rain – Threshold Choir
The Healer's Way Volumes 1 & 2 – Stella Benson

Web Sites of Interest

http://www.deathmidwifery.com – Create Sacred Space for Conscious Transitions – our web site

http://groups.google.com/group/deathmidwifery - The Art of Death Midwifery discussion group

http://www.meditationiseasy.com – Meditation

http://www.hemi-sync.com – Monroe Institute's series of music to navigate levels of consciousness

http://www.chaliceofrepose.org - Music thanatology

http://www.growthhouse.org/music.html - Music thanatology

http://www.healingmusic.org - Healing music and information

http://www.thresholdchoir.org - Women's choral group dedicated to singing for the dying

http://www. psychopomp.org – Information on the history of death guides

http://www.getpalliativecare.org – Palliative care

http://www.hospicenet.org – Hospice

http://www.centerforloss.com - Alan Wolfelt's bereavement center

http://www.caringinfo.org – Information on grieving

http://www.alternativefuneralmonitor.com – Alternative funerals

http://www.finalpassages.org – Home funerals

http://www.greenburials.org – Green burials

http://www.uslivingwillregistry.com – Living wills

http://www.nlm.nih.gov/medlineplus/advancedirectives.html - Advance directives

INDEX

CPSIA information can be obtained at www.ICGtesting.com
Printed in the USA
LVOW06s0052290514

387629LV00001B/162/P

9 781439 229064